To: Pastor Smedley,

May God Grant you continued Favor and many more years of Great health to continue Serving and blessing others. Thank you for all the years of support and encouragement.

Spiritual Gifts

"Unveiling Your Inner Light"

Blessings,
Yvonne Allen

Written By: Yvonne Allen

Printed in United States of America

Copyright © 2014 by Yvonne Allen. All rights reserved. No part of this publication may be reproduced, stored in a retrieval system, or transmitted in any form or by any means, electronic, mechanical, photocopy, recording or otherwise, without consent of the publisher. Please direct your inquiries to Forester & Cohen

Publishing at: info@cohenpublishing.com

United States Copyright Office Registration No. Pending

Library of Congress Cataloging-in-Publication Data has been applied for

ISBN: 978-0-9839422-2-1

Cover Design by SanCrew.com

Editor: Tiffany Exum

Forester & Cohen Publishing, LLC

5257 Buckeystown Pike, Suite 423

Frederick, Maryland 21704

CohenPublishing.com

Table of Content

I am Saved, So Now What? 5

Spiritual Gifts 11

Definitions of each Gift.. 25

Places To Use Your Spiritual Gifts 47

What is my Purpose? 51

What are the Some Basic Life Principles 57

Good versus Evil 59

How You Can Survive a Satanic Attack 69

Prayer Changes things 75

Situational Prayers.. 87

CHAPTER 1
I am Saved, So Now What?

I was just saved and turned my life over to Christ, "Now What" is an important question...

I'm so afraid that many new converts are faced with this question "I am saved, now what?" and often end up going back to exactly the same lifestyle because they do not understand the changes they must make in their lives. They don't know what to do after they have given their lives over to Christ. Sadly, Christianity has come down to saying a simple, little prayer. That is not what God intended for us. I would like to give you some guidance around what to do next, after you are saved.

So, you felt the Holy Spirit tugging on your heart to make a change in your life and you listened? Good for you! Now what do you do? Your decision to receive Christ as Savior is the most important decision you will ever make. There is no greater joy in all the world than to know Christ personally; to know your sins are forgiven and you have peace in your soul. You have been born again! Born of the Spirit! A miracle has taken place in your life. Now it's time to begin to spend time with people that are striving to live a Godly life so that you can help each other grow. Godly relationships are essential for growing in Christ; you become like the people you hang around. I Corinthians 15:33 says it like this; "Bad company corrupts good morals." Develop relationships with people who will help you spiritually.

As you attend church, you will find opportunities to be involved with others of the same spirit. Take advantage of the opportunity and get involved. Don't think of the church as a building; think of the church as a community. It is very important that believers in Jesus Christ fellowship with one another. That is one of the primary purposes of the church. I strongly encourage you to find a Bible-believing church in your area and speak to the pastor. Let him know about your new faith in Jesus Christ.

Spiritual Gifts

Unveiling Your Inner Light

The last thing you want to do is plant yourself in a place where you will not grow. Look at it this way, you will not find a peach or orange tree planted in Alaska, will you? Why not? It will die because it does not receive the essential life giving aspects that this particular tree needs to grow. The same goes for Christians. Plant yourself in a church that will preach and teach the Word in a clear, relevant, powerful way, so that you can receive the essential life giving aspects you need to grow as a Christian.

In order to grow to maturity as a Christian, you must be loyal and obedient to the commands of Christ. He said, "If you love me, keep my commandments." (John 14:15). Some of these requirements are listed so that you may know what our Lord expects of His disciples.

1. Be Baptized

Baptism is simply a step of obedience, a public proclamation of your faith in Christ alone for salvation. If you are ready to be baptized, you should speak with a pastor. Baptism is the first step of obedience for a new Christian. The first public act in the ministry of Jesus was His baptism by John the Baptist in the river Jordan (Matthew 3:13-17). Baptism is an outward sign of the old, sinful man being dead and buried, as you are submerged under the water, and the birth of a new creation, the new man in Christ as you break through the surface of the water as and rise to a new way of living! Baptism alone, does not save you, but it shows others you are saved and now want to follow the ways of a Christian.

2. Read Your Bible Daily

It is very important for us to spend time each day focusing on God. Some people call this a "quiet time." Others call it "devotions," because it is a time when we devote ourselves to God. Some prefer to set aside time in the mornings, while others prefer the evenings. It does not matter what you call this time or when you do it. What matters is that you regularly spend time with God. What events make up our time with God? In addition to being taught the Bible in church, Sunday school, and/or Bible studies – you need to be reading the Bible for yourself.

The Bible contains everything you need to know to live a successful Christian life. It contains God's guidance about how to make wise decisions, how to know God's will, how to minister to others, and how to grow spiritually. The Bible is God's Word to us. The Bible is essentially God's instruction manual for how to live our lives in a way that is pleasing to Him and satisfying to us. Just as you need physical food in order to sustain physical life, you need spiritual food (the Bible) to maintain spiritual life. I suggest you begin with the New Testament, reading the Gospel of John or Mark. Follow this with the book of Acts. Next, read Paul's Epistle to the Romans. The entire New Testament can be read in three months by reading three chapters a day. By reading three chapters of the Old Testament and one chapter of the New Testament each day, the whole Bible can be read in one year. I suggest you set aside a few moments at the beginning of each day for Bible study. Look for promises to claim, commandments to obey, examples to follow and sins to avoid. Memorize key verses, such as John 3:16. Your growth as a Christian will be directly related to your personal application of the Word of God.

3. Pray Every Day

Prayer is simply talking to God. Talk to God about your concerns and problems. Ask God to give you wisdom and guidance. Ask God to provide for your needs. Tell God how much you love Him and how much you appreciate all He does for you. This is what prayer is all about. Forget the "Thee's and "Thou's" and just talk to God like you would talk to a friend. HE IS LISTENING. Begin with worship. Tell Him you love Him. Thank Him for all He has done, ask Him for the strength and help you need to live for Jesus Christ, then, tell Him what your needs are. Prayer is between you and the Father. Prayer is a must for the Christian life. Pray when you are tempted to do wrong. Pray for your needs. Prayer is also thanksgiving and praise. Start a prayer list. Write down your prayer needs on paper or in your Bible. Then, as the Lord answers your prayer, scratch it off your list. The answers will be either yes, no or wait. If the answer is no, it is because God is protecting you or he has something better in store for you. Remember, "... ye have not because ye ask not" (James 4:2). There is nothing too great and nothing too small to take to the Lord in prayer.

4. Witness for Christ

Try to find a friend or two, perhaps from your church, who can help you and encourage you (Hebrews 3:13; 10:24). Ask your friends to keep you accountable in regard to your quiet time, your activities, and your walk with God. Ask if you can do the same for them. This does not mean you have to give up all your friends who do not know the Lord Jesus as their Savior.

Continue to be their friend and love them. Simply let them know that Jesus has changed your life and you cannot do all the same things you used to do. Ask God to give you opportunities to share Jesus with your friends. The greatest work in the world is soul winning, and every Christian can and should bring others to the Savior. Jesus said, "Ye shall be a witness unto Me." (Acts 1:8). Try to speak naturally and cheerfully every day to someone about Christ. Remember that you witness by what you do as well as by what you say. At home, at work, and at school, there should be something about you that's different; love, patience, and understanding. Tell someone about Jesus Christ who made the difference.

5. Tithe Your Income

The Lord's work needs your support and help. You need to give your time, work, and money to help in the Lord's work. As you give, you will learn that the Lord gives to you. "Give and it shall be given unto you..." (Luke 6:38). A good Christian should volunteer and look for ways to be used of God. At least the tithe (one tenth) of your income should be given freely to the Lord. It is a blessing to give as the Lord gives to us (Matthew 6:33). Tithing (giving one-tenth) of your income is the Biblical method of supporting God's work. The Bible tells us, "Upon the first day of the week (Sunday) let every one of you lay by him in store, as God hath prospered him." (I Corinthians 16:2). God says to bring the tithe into the "storehouse," meaning the local church. Your church is your storehouse of spiritual food, blessing and service, so this is the proper place to give your tithe. "Bring ye all the tithes into the storehouse and prove me now herewith, saith the Lord of Hosts, if I will not open you the windows of Heaven and pour you out a blessing, that there shall not be room enough to receive it." (Malachi 3:10). The right use of money is a test of character. If you are dishonest to God in money matters, you cannot grow spiritually.

6. Attend Church Regularly

The Christian life is not just our own private affair; it is to be a family affair, in which we enjoy the fellowship with our Heavenly Father and with each other. Every Christian should unite with a local, Bible believing church and share its worship, its fellowship, and its witness. If Jesus loved the church enough to die for it (Ephesians 5:25), then we should love and support it. Regular church attendance should be as much of a habit as eating. "Not forsaking the assembling of ourselves together" (Hebrews 10:25) is a clear command of the word of God. At the church services, you will hear God's word read, explained, and applied to your everyday problems in life. God has ordained (set aside) men to minister and preach His Word. Every Christian, young and old, needs the inspiration and information gained in a church worship service. If you try to live the Christian life alone, failure will result. In unity, there is strength. Through the church, you can render service to a lost and dying world.

7. Stop Living the Way You Used to Live

I am not sure what kind of lifestyle you had before coming to know Christ, but as a Christian, we are called to live a Godly life. Christians ARE NOT perfect. We do, however, ask God for His forgiveness when we mess up or make a mistake, and then seek His Word for strength, guidance, and wisdom so we do not make that same mistake again. Although your decision to become a Christian is great and important, it is not all you need. It is but the beginning of a new life in

Christ. When you were saved, you were not immediately a full grown Christian, but a "babe in Christ." As a baby Christian, you are commanded to "grow" (II Peter 3:18). Everyone loves babies, but no one wants them to stay in the nursery. Only by growing spiritually can you please God and glorify Him in your life. In order to grow to maturity as a Christian, you must be loyal and obedient to the commands of Christ.

Spiritual Gifts

Unveiling Your Inner Light

8. Use Your Spiritual Gifts

A spiritual gift is a "God-given" assignment, capacity, and desire to perform a function within the body of Christ with supernatural joy, energy, and effectiveness. "What do you enjoy most about serving the Lord?" You will look forward to the responsibilities you are given that call on you to use your gift. On the other hand, you will not be as motivated for tasks that are outside your giftedness. When we minister to others through our gifts, we are tapping into the inexhaustible energy and motivation of God. We experience an extra measure of energy and joy. God chooses your gift(s); He alone decides. He doesn't give you a "gift card" so you can pick the ones you want. You don't get to choose your gift. You can only choose to "unveil" your gift and use it. The good news is that you don't have to earn your gift either!

Serving outside our gifts is a different story altogether. I believe this is the primary reason why so many Christians burn out on church work. Instead of finding a position where they can use their gifts, they sign up for whatever task is available. They do their best as long as they can take it, then they quit. To discover your spiritual gifts you can take spiritual gifts tests. However, the best way to discover your gift would probably be to serve in a variety of ministry situations. When you find the area that suits your gift, you will know it. Along with your gift(s) will also come a divinely inspired desire to exercise that gift. As you begin to apply your spiritual gift, your motivation will become more and more "want" rather than "ought to" or "have to!" The gifts give direction and purpose in life!

There is far more to the Christian life than what is included here however, if these initial steps are carefully followed, I believe you will find yourself growing more in the knowledge of our Lord and Savior Jesus Christ.

CHAPTER 2
Spiritual Gifts

Have you felt purposeless in life? Beliefs about God's plans for our individual lives vary. Some believe that God has given us certain gifts and talents to steward, but does not have a specific job, specific spouse, or specific direction for us. Others believe that God has a detailed plan for every moment or aspect of life. One thing is certain: God has placed a call on each of us. Whether it is His general call to all believers, the gifts He has given us, or a more specific plan, God has a purpose for our lives. Discovering your spiritual gifts plays a major role in finding your purpose.

Spiritual gifts are abilities God gives the believer for the purpose of service. They are not human talents. Human talents are inadequate to do the work of God. For though we walk in the flesh, we do not war according to the flesh. For the weapons of our warfare are not carnal but mighty in God for pulling down strongholds (2 Corinthians 10:3,4).

Spiritual gifts are either supernatural abilities that God has bestowed on individuals, or God-given natural abilities that function through the direction of the Holy Spirit. Gifts such as miracles, tongues, healing, and prophecy are supernatural in origin. Other spiritual gifts, such as teaching, administration, and helps, are God-given abilities to perform a particular role in Gods program. Though nonbelievers may have the same abilities, they do not function under the direction of the Holy Spirit. The Holy Spirit takes these God-given abilities and uses them for His purposes in the lives of believers. Therefore, the gifts of the Spirit are abilities, either natural or supernatural, given by God for the work of the ministry. The Bible says that all gifts ultimately have their source in God.

We have different gifts, according to the grace given to each of us. If your gift is prophesying, then prophesy in accordance with your faith; if it is serving, then serve; if it is teaching, then teach; if it is to encourage, then

Spiritual Gifts

Unveiling Your Inner Light

give encouragement; if it is giving, then give generously; if it is to lead, do it diligently; if it is to show mercy, do it cheerfully. (Romans 12:6-8)

Every good gift and perfect gift is from above, and comes down from the Father of lights, with whom there is no variation or shadow of turning (James 1:17).

Each one of us has been given gifts by the Holy Spirit. We can use these gifts to live in peace with God's purpose for our lives. We can employ these gifts to take our place and be an active part in God's wonderful plan for the world. Our choice is simple. We have the wonderful invitation to be a part of God's work in reconciling and reuniting the world. When we work towards that cause, we are God's people.

God wants you to use your gifts to live out His plan for your life. Because you have particular gifts as a unique child of God, your gifts influence the specific ways in which you respond to God's call in your life. Your gifts shape the way you live your life.

How can the gifts of the Holy Spirit within you bring you joy? As you use and live within the gifts of God, you'll have a sense of doing what you were created to do and being who you were created to be. You'll affirm your best self, as God planned for you to be. You'll find satisfaction and happiness as you do particular things well. You'll act on your values and beliefs. You'll see your deepest longings and hopes fulfilled as you use your gifts effectively to achieve realistic goals. God may ask you to stretch your potential, but God will not ask you to do things that you are not equipped or called to do. Remember, each gifts can be lived out in a number of ways.

As you use your gifts, you will begin to understand that reaching your potential is more important than reaching the goal or goals you have set for yourself. If you are successful by the world's standards but are unfaithful to what is true and right and of God, then you will fail in your efforts as a disciple. As you discern and use your gifts, you will enter an exciting experience of self- discovery. You'll find new opportunities to use the full potential of your life. It is exciting to know that you can be a part of God's plan to renew the world.

Spiritual Gifts

Unveiling Your Inner Light

Knowing our gifts help us to know where to place our time and energy. We begin to prioritize our tasks and jobs; no longer feeling overcome by the thought that everything is of equal importance to serve God and the community. Identifying our gifts and telling others what our gifts are help us to say "no". In this way we can have the time and resources available to say "yes" when we can contribute our very best.

When we accomplish a task or project that we know God has called and equipped us to do, we feel good about the work and ourselves. Our self- esteem is lifted and we find pleasure in the dignity of our work, the elegance of its simplicity, and the essential responsibility in serving others. Of course, if we over use our gifts and don't take care of ourselves, burnout could be a result.

When we minister to others through our gifts, we are tapping into the inexhaustible energy and motivation of God. When we exercise our gifts, the Holy Spirit works through us. Every child of God has at least one spiritual gift and no one has them all. One way to discover your gifts is to take spiritual gifts tests. However probably the best way to discover your gift is to serve in a variety of ministry situations. When you find the area that suits your gift, you will know it. Romans 12:3-8, 1Corinthians 12:4-11, 1Corinthians 12:27-31, Ephesians 4:7-16

If you would like to take a spiritual gifts test, I have one that is pretty accurate. I have used this test myself and at many conventions, workshops, seminars and churches. Please take the test first, before you read the definitions of each gift to be more accurate. I find that people who read the definitions before they take the test will answer their questions differently because they would like to have a particular gift. For example, I would love to have the gift of healing and prophecy, but I don't and might answer the questions in a way that might sway the way I respond to the questions because I want to have those particular gifts. My point is, take the test below first before you read any further.

Rank each of the following statements as it applies to your experience or inclination. There is no right or wrong answer. Be honest with yourself,

Spiritual Gifts   _____

Unveiling Your Inner Light

that way you can have some idea and/or know your spiritual gifts from God. Please be sure to let your responses reflect your opinions of yourself.

A Lot (3)   Some (2)   Little (1)   None (0).

1. ____I make a point to be with people of other cultures and ethnic backgrounds.

2. ____I See destructive patterns in people's lives and help them to find healthier ways of living

3. ____I listen as other people tell me about their religious experiences and spiritual journeys.

4. ____People often seek me out and ask me to pray with them.

5. ____I can explain in simple ways complex ideas about God and how to live as a disciple.

6. ____I often praise coworkers or friends for their good work and attitude.

7. ____I carefully get all the information I need before moving into action.

8. ____I can share deep truths with others about their problems.

9. ____When I see a need, I spring to action and do something about it.

10. ____I am materially blessed, and I give what I can to others freely.

11. ____Being in charge doesn't mean I have to control everything.

12. ____I can sit and simply listen to someone who needs a listening ear.

13. ____I do the best I can and leave the rest in God's hands.

14. ____I speak up and tell others when I don't believe they are telling the whole truth.

15. ____I have experienced times when something miraculously happened that was contrary to natural law.

Spiritual Gifts

Unveiling Your Inner Light

16. ____I look for opportunities to bring hope and God's comfort to those who are sick.

17. ____I have spoken in verbal utterances that praise God but are not understandable by human ear.

18. ____I have been able to learn foreign languages easily.

19. ____My circle of friends are so many, it looks like a meeting of the United Nations.

20. ____I am energized when I speak about what needs to be changed in church and other arenas.

21. ____Inviting others to join me in something I enjoy is something I do every week.

22. ____I find myself time and again listening to people's spiritual struggles and offering guidance.

23. ____When I am a student in a class or the teacher of a class, other participants are energized and motivated.

24. ____I am able to work with people and help them do their best.

25. ____I am able to grasp deep truths about God and make sense of them.

26. ____I am able to use my knowledge in complex situations, weighing the pros and cons, and know what is right.

27. ____I don't mind lending a hand and doing the trivial jobs that are often overlooked.

28. ____I give 10% of my income and more to my church and other charitable needs.

29. ____When I am working on a group project, I make the extra effort to communicate with everyone.

Spiritual Gifts

Unveiling Your Inner Light

30. ____Stopping what I am doing to help someone in need is a normal part of my day.

31. ____When I believe that something is of God, I act boldly on my belief.

32. ____My friends often ask me to help sort out what is real and what is phony.

33. ____God has mysteriously intervened in extraordinary ways in my presence.

34. ____I am able to counsel others to help restore them to mental and spiritual health.

35. ____I have spoken in a language that I am not normally able to speak.

36. ____I can hear verbal sounds not understood by others and understand what is meant.

37. ____I rejoice that our church has such a wide diversity of people.

38. ____I can see change coming and am not afraid to help people make the needed changes.

39. ____Sharing how I became a Christian comes naturally for me.

40. ____I can be called upon when someone needs help in making difficult decisions.

41. ____I am good at giving directions to people so that they can complete projects successfully.

42. ____I make a point to say a kind word to those whose abilities I admire.

43. ____I am deeply satisfied when I study in order to explain hard concepts to others.

Spiritual Gifts

Unveiling Your Inner Light

44. ____I don't panic in difficult situations, but weigh all the circumstances to find a solution.

45. ____I'd rather stay in the background doing the labor than be out front speaking or teaching.

46. ____I spend a lot of time earning and raising money and an equal amount of time giving it away.

47. ____I am good at organizing and leading a group to meet their goals.

48. ____I walk gently with people who are grieving, and can walk with them in their process of healing.

49. ____I live the best I can each day, one day at a time, not worry about tomorrow.

50. ____I can "see through" people and circumstances and know what is real and what is not.

51. ____Time and again I have seen miracles, acts contrary to natural law, occur.

52. ____I am able to help, comfort, and counsel when people are deeply troubled.

53. ____I have had the experience of "speaking in tongues."

54. ____I am able to move into another culture, speak another language, and feel at home.

After you have answered all the questions, transfer your answers from the questions sheet to your answer sheet. Add the total at the end of each line, starting from left to right. Also take into consideration that this test reflects only your past history and not what God may be doing, even now, in this moment, or will do in your future. God gives gifts to everyone and distributes them according to his grace.

Spiritual Gifts _____

Unveiling Your Inner Light

Spiritual Gifts Answer Sheet Below:

Gift	Responses			Total
Apostleship	1 ____	19 ____	37 ____	____
Prophecy	2 ____	20 ____	38 ____	____
Evangelism	3 ____	21 ____	39 ____	____
Pastoring	4 ____	22 ____	40 ____	____
Teaching	5 ____	23 ____	41 ____	____
Exhortation	6 ____	24 ____	42 ____	____
Knowledge	7 ____	25 ____	43 ____	____
Wisdom	8 ____	26 ____	44 ____	____
Service	9 ____	27 ____	45 ____	____
Giving	10 ____	28 ____	46 ____	____
Leadership	11 ____	29 ____	47 ____	____
Mercy	12 ____	30 ____	48 ____	____
Faith	13 ____	31 ____	49 ____	____
Discernment	14 ____	32 ____	50 ____	____
Miracles	15 ____	33 ____	51 ____	____
Healing	16 ____	34 ____	52 ____	____
Tongues	17 ____	35 ____	53 ____	____
Interpretation	18 ____	36 ____	54 ____	____

After you have totaled them all side to side (not up and down), look

Spiritual Gifts

Unveiling Your Inner Light

at each line. When the totals add up to nine there is a very strong chance that is your spiritual gift. If you don't have any nines then go to the eights, and so on and so forth. Once you look at the gifts associated with all of your nines or eights, you should have an idea of what your gifts are. We are only human, so in order to know what your gifts truly are, pray and ask God to give you spiritual insight into your gift. That way you will know for yourself.

Below is a sample of the questions and answer sheet filled out to help you understand the instructions given:

1. __2__ I make a point to be with people of other cultures and ethnic backgrounds.

2. __3__ I See destructive patterns in people's lives and help them to find healthier ways of living

3. __3__ I listen as other people tell me about their religious experiences and spiritual journeys.

4. __1__ People often seek me out and ask me to pray with them.

5. __1__ I can explain in simple ways complex ideas about God and how to live as a disciple.

6. __3__ I often praise coworkers or friends for their good work and attitude.

7. __2__ I carefully get all the information I need before moving into action.

8. __3__ I can share deep truths with others about their problems.

9. __2__ When I see a need, I spring to action and do something about it.

10. __3__ I am materially blessed, and I give what I can to others freely.

11. __0__ Being in charge doesn't mean I have to control everything.

Spiritual Gifts

Unveiling Your Inner Light

12. __3__ I can sit and simply listen to someone who needs a listening ear.

13. __3__ I do the best I can and leave the rest in God's hands.

14. __1__ I speak up and tell others when I don't believe they are telling the whole truth.

15. __1__ I have experienced times when something miraculously happened that was contrary to natural law.

16. __1__ I look for opportunities to bring hope and God's comfort to those who are sick.

17. __1__ I have spoken in verbal utterances that praise God but are not understandable by human ear.

18. __0__ I have been able to learn foreign languages easily.

19. __1__ My circle of friends are so many, it looks like a meeting of the United Nations.

20. __0__ I am energized when I speak about what needs to be changed in church and other arenas.

21. __2__ Inviting others to join me in something I enjoy is something I do every week.

22. __0__ I find myself time and again listening to people's spiritual struggles and offering guidance.

23. __0__ When I am a student in a class or the teacher of a class, other participants are energized and motivated.

24. __3__ I am able to work with people and help them do their best.

25. __1__ I am able to grasp deep truths about God and make sense of them.

26. __2__ I am able to use my knowledge in complex situations, weighing the pros and cons, and know what is right.

Spiritual Gifts

Unveiling Your Inner Light

27. __3__ I don't mind lending a hand and doing the trivial jobs that are often overlooked.

28. __3__ I give 10% of my income and more to my church and other charitable needs.

29. __2__ When I am working on a group project, I make the extra effort to communicate with everyone.

30. __3__ Stopping what I am doing to help someone in need is a normal part of my day.

31. __3__ When I believe that something is of God, I act boldly on my belief.

18

32. __3__ My friends often ask me to help sort out what is real and what is phony.

33. __3__ God has mysteriously intervened in extraordinary ways in my presence.

34. __3__ I am able to counsel others to help restore them to mental and spiritual health.

35. __0__ I have spoken in a language that I am not normally able to speak.

36. __0__ I can hear verbal sounds not understood by others and understand what is meant.

37. __0__ I rejoice that our church has such a wide diversity of people.

38. __3__ I can see change coming and am not afraid to help people make the needed changes.

39. __2__ Sharing how I became a Christian comes naturally for me.

40. __3__ I can be called upon when someone needs help in making difficult decisions.

Spiritual Gifts

Unveiling Your Inner Light

41. __3__ I am good at giving directions to people so that they can complete projects successfully.

42. __3__ I make a point to say a kind word to those whose abilities I admire.

43. __3__ I am deeply satisfied when I study in order to explain hard concepts to others.

44. __1__ I don't panic in difficult situations, but weigh all the circumstances to find a solution.

45. __3__ I'd rather stay in the background doing the labor than be out front speaking or teaching.

46. __2__ I spend a lot of time earning and raising money and an equal amount of time giving it away.

47. __1__ I am good at organizing and leading a group to meet their goals.

48. __1__ I walk gently with people who are grieving, and can walk with them in their process of healing.

49. __0__ I live the best I can each day, one day at a time, not worry about tomorrow.

50. __3__ I can "see through" people and circumstances and know what is real and what is not.

51. __2__ Time and again I have seen miracles, acts contrary to natural law, occur.

52. __3__ I am able to help, comfort, and counsel when people are deeply troubled.

53. __0__ I have had the experience of "speaking in tongues."

54. __0__ I am able to move into another culture, speak another language, and feel at home.

Spiritual Gifts

Unveiling Your Inner Light

Spiritual Gifts Answer Sheet Sample Completed Below Taken From The Questions Sheet:

Gift	Responses			Total
Apostleship	1 _2_	19 _1_	37 _0_	_3_
Prophecy	2 _3_	20 _0_	38 _3_	_6_
Evangelism	3 _3_	21 _2_	39 _2_	_7_
Pastoring	4 _1_	22 _0_	40 _3_	_4_
Teaching	5 _1_	23 _0_	41 _3_	_4_
Exhortation	6 _3_	24 _3_	42 _3_	_9_ ***
Knowledge	7 _2_	25 _1_	43 _3_	_6_
Wisdom	8 _3_	26 _2_	44 _1_	_6_
Service	9 _2_	27 _3_	45 _3_	_8_ **
Giving	10 _3_	28 _3_	46 _2_	_8_ **
Leadership	11 _0_	29 _2_	47 _1_	_3_
Mercy	12 _3_	30 _3_	48 _1_	_7_
Faith	13 _3_	31 _3_	49 _0_	_6_
Discernment	14 _1_	32 _3_	50 _3_	_7_
Miracles	15 _1_	33 _3_	51 _2_	_6_
Healing	16 _1_	34 _3_	52 _3_	_7_
Tongues	17 _1_	35 _0_	53 _0_	_1_
Interpretation	18 _0_	36 _0_	54 _0_	_0_

As you can see, the totals are side to side (not up and down). As I stated before, when the totals add up to nine there is a very strong chance that is your spiritual gift. The person that completed the sample test is actually a friend of mine, Kristy. I happen to know that she has all three of the gifts that are highlighted above. The nine indicated that she has exhortation and the eights indicated she also has service and giving, which I know to be true.

Also, as a guide for you, I have listed in the next chapter definitions of each gift with biblical references underneath each spiritual gift to help you understand your true gift. Once you read each spiritual gift definition, you should know whether this applies to you or not.

CHAPTER 3
Definitions of Each Gift

Discerning of Spirits: "The special ability to know with assurance whether certain behavior purported to be of God is in reality divine, human, or Satanic." Christians with this gift can recognize the true motives of people and also recognize when a person is distorting the truth or communicating error. This person often can recognize when Satan or other evil spirits are at work in a given person or situation. Scriptures: Matthew 16:21-23; Acts 5:1-11; 16:16-18; 17:11-16; 1 Corinthians 12:10; Hebrews 5:14; 1 John 4:1-6.

I would like to share with you my experience with the gift of discernment or as some bible variations call it; distinguishing between spirits. When I was about 13 years old, my parents lived in a house in Wisconsin that had many bad spirits. I didn't know anything about spiritual gifts until I was a little older. It's because of my discernment capabilities and gifts I was able to pick up on bad spirits in the house. I could see the shadows, feel them all around me, and I recognized that they were spirits that were bad and should not be in this house. No one else in my family had this gift. When I tried to explain to them that there was something wrong, they just laughed and said I was crazy. They thought it was all in my mind. Even though I did not know there was such a thing as a spiritual gift, I would speak to those evil spirits; let them know that I do know that they were there, and that I recognize that they were bad spirits. I would also tell them to leave me alone and get out of my house; that I was a child of God in that they could not touch me.

This was an ongoing thing for me. At one point, I even started to believe my parents and friends and thought to myself, "maybe I am crazy". I did not know what was going on or even what was happening to me spiritually. I would hear things, like footsteps of someone running through the house; the lights would go on and off; the TV and radio would come on by itself. I would hear something running up and down the stairs. I could

Spiritual Gifts _____

Unveiling Your Inner Light

feel and see shadows of the spirits actually passing me. As a teenager, this was very frightening and even scarier not knowing what was really going on.

It had gotten to the point where I was not only angry with myself because I did not know what was going on; I was angry with God. When the spirits were really bad and I could feel and see them everywhere, I would cry out to God and ask "why is this happening to me?" At this point, I was so frustrated that I ask my parents to consider taking me to see a psychiatrist because there is something truly wrong with me. This went on for years.

One day by the grace of God, one of my uncles who had the gift of prophecy and discernment came by the house. He walked through the house making the same statements that I made and telling to my mom that something was wrong in this house. It made me feel really good to know that someone else felt the same way I felt. He would walk through the house and started saying "what is going on here? You have some really bad spirits in this house. Don't you see them here? Don't you hear them? In fact, you have Satan himself sitting right in your living room. This is very bad. We're going to have to pray the evil spirits out of this house immediately. How in the world are you able to sleep at night or even walk around during the day with all of these bad spirits?" I was relieved and said to myself, "Thank God I'm not the only one that feels that way. Thank God someone else understands what I am going through." My uncle immediately started

praying, walking through the house saying," I rebuke any spirit that is not of God and I cast you in the most outer a part of the sea. You will leave this house! Get out now in the name of Jesus." After that moment, everything that I felt bad in that house went away. I no longer heard footsteps, doors slamming or saw shadows anymore. That made me feel really good and from that point on I started researching the bible. That's when I found out that there were such things as spiritual gifts. I was about 15 years old. That was over 35 years ago. Of course, I did not understand why God gave me that gift because it was so scary to me to be able to recognize and see demons. Now that I'm older, of course, I do understand. I could go on for pages and probably write several books on discernment

Spiritual Gifts

Unveiling Your Inner Light

alone and have so many examples throughout my life of my experience with negative forces and demons but I will not because we need to focus on God and not demons. My spiritual gift of discernment is really quite interesting now that I totally understand it. Not only am I able to feel negative spirits when I walk into a house or a building if they are present but also if I happen to shake someone's hand I can feel whether their spirit is of God or of Satan. Trust me, this is not a good feeling. I will only take someone's hand if I am being polite and introducing myself only if it is absolutely necessary because I don't like the feeling I get when he is negative. There have been times when I look someone in the eyes and I can see the demonic spirits present. Because I don't like the way it feels, I usually look at them, turn and walk the other direction. I don't want to deal with that. Those spirits that are not of God know that I recognized and can see them for who they really are. I am sure they are happy when I just turn and walk away and don't call them out. They aren't as happy as I am because I don't I have to deal with it. And I walk away rebuking them in the name of Jesus.

My friends who know that I have this spiritual gift of discernment are always asking me to either check out a building or a new apartment that they are moving into or even a new house that they want to move into. So usually because they are children of Christ, my friend, and understand the spiritual gifts, I will do this for them. If I feel anything that is not of God I usually let them know and they can do one of two things. They can either not move into a house or we together can pray these evil spirits out of this house. Most of the time they just don't move into the house. If they have already moved into a house and ask me to come over, I walk the house to see if I feel anything. If I do feel something that's not of God, we just pray and rebuke any spirit and ask them to leave. I have gone as far as to open the door and windows and demand those evil spirits to get out. I tell my friends this is something I cannot control. This is a gift that only God can control, not a magic wand that I just wave in front of them and magic happens. This has to come from the Holy Spirit and God. I tell them this is not something I can turn on or off, it comes from god. My friends still insists that I walk through the house and get those spirits out of there if they are present. So, what I usually do is pray before I enter the house that God will reveal that truth and remove any spirit that's not of God and he does.

Another experience I have met with discernment has happened when God was protecting me from someone who was trying to deceive me. They have been many times when I was talking to someone and they would say something to me and deep inside the spirit would tell me not to believe them. The spirit would say something like "don't be deceived they are not telling you the truth" and because I am stunned from hearing that from of the spirit, and overwhelmed from hearing that, I cannot say anything at that time. Sometimes when I hear the spirit tell me that this person is trying to deceive, me I don't pause I just blurt out the words "you are lying to me." That usually gets me into trouble with that person because they usually asked me to a prove it and I cannot. I only know what the spirit just told me about that person. How can I prove it? Now that I have a lot more experience hearing from the Holy Spirit when someone is lying to me and the Holy Spirit told me, I keep my mouth shut and just know for myself they are lying and God is just protecting me. That truly is a wonderful thing to have. I am blessed.

Whenever I see the advertisement on television promoting those demonic movies, I really get upset because people have no idea that Demons are real and are walking this earth causing havoc and chaos among people. If you think because the producers of these films mention that these demons are fiction and you don't know God you will believe this is not real so if this happens on film and it is pretend. Then if you happen to have an encounter or an experience in real life with a demon you would think that your mind is playing games on you and it is all in your head and not real because of what you have seen at the movies. I really feel sorry for people who don't know God and don't know that demons are very real. The only way you can really understand about them is to study the word of God. A spiritual warfare going on as we speak. Only through prayer can God fight those battles for you.

Exhortation:

"The special ability to minister words of comfort, consolation, encouragement, and counsel to other people in such a way that they feel helped and healed". Those who use this gift within a teaching situation are often driven to give practical application to their insights. Often, those gifted in this gift desire step-by-step plans of action to help others. Exhorters often find it natural to discover insights from personal experience. Scriptures: Luke 3:16-18; Acts 11:23; 14:22; Romans 12:8; 1 Timothy 4:12; 5:1; Hebrews 10:25. Exhortation focuses on personal and practical application of the message or truth being communicated. And the message or truth being communicated.

I have two friends who have the gift of exhortation. Some variations of the bible refer to exhortation as encouragement. The people who have the gift of exhortation are really good at encouraging others. It comes naturally to them and they are very good at it. Once in a while we all get discouraged at some point in our lives, or even worse, depressed. The spirit of depression is not from God as you know. It is a demonic spirit that is used to keep you from seeing your blessing. Sometimes this spirit will come upon me and I have a difficult time shaking it off. I then will call upon my friends or people I know who have the gift of exhortation because I know they are very good at lifting my spirits. Most of the time they tell me things that I already know. It is just that Satan wants me to focus on the negative to try in keep me down. Remember it tells you in the bible that Satan's purpose is to steal, kill and destroy. One of Satan's tactics is to steal your joy by telling you no one cares and to get you to focus on the things you don't have in life. He wants you to focus on anything that is a negative such as finances, health; relationships so on and so forth.

Faith:

"The special ability that God gives certain members of the Body of Christ to discern with extraordinary confidence the will and purposes of God for His work." Those with this gift often scare other people with their confidence. People with this gift are often very irritated by criticism, as they consider it to be criticism against God and His will. Probably the biggest danger for those with this gift is that they often try to project their gift onto other people. Scriptures: Acts 11:22-24; 27:21-25; Romans 4:18-21; 1 Corinthians 12:9; Hebrews 11.

Spiritual Gifts _____

Unveiling Your Inner Light

Both my husband and my brother Joe have the gift of faith. I have a good friend who has the gift of faith as well. In every church, the pastors constantly preach about having faith. There is a difference in staying faithful or having faith in God that he will turn the situation around in your favor and the gift of faith itself. Most people seem to get that confused. People with the gift of faith usually get very irritated and frustrated when they know you should have faith in God and believe that he will come through for you that he will carry you through the storm. My husband for example, gets very frustrated with me if I get down or depressed about a certain situation because he believes that if I am a child of God and believe that God will do what the bible says he will do, how can I ever get down or depressed, from his point of view. Because of this I try not to tell him that I am worried or afraid about something. When he hears it in my voice or if I happen to say I am worried about a situation he gets upset with me and says "as much as you read the bible and study different books and get others' spiritual advice, how in the world can you believe or think that God would not fix this situation? What in the world is the matter with you? I know he is right about having faith in God but at the same time, when I am going through a difficult situation, I really just want him to encourage me instead of basically telling me I should know better than to think that God has forgotten about me.

On the other hand, when I know that someone is going through something and they need a person with the gift of faith that can explain the promises of God and the fact that if you have faith and stay in the word of God, he will work out all your problems before you know what it; I will refer them to my husband or my friends. They can be very helpful in a situation like that. Now, my brother Joe on the other hand, when he was alive, would be encouraging and trying to get me to believe that God is going to work it out. He used always tell me not to look at the negative side of it, look at what God can do and will do on a positive note. He used to tell me "stop worrying about everything God worked it out in the past, don't you think that he knows what's going to happen in the future? He knows before you know so don't worry about anything." This is something I knew about him so I knew not to go to him with my problems, being down or thinking negative thoughts because he would get irritated and ask me why would I do such a thing when, God that is accessible 24 hours a day and give you anything that you ask of Him if it is His will. People who have the gift of faith, are not truly judging anyone, they just don't understand how you don't have faith enough to believe and know what they believe; that God will not leave you or forsake you.

Giving:

"The special ability that God gives to certain members of the Body of Christ to contribute their material resources to the work of the Lord with liberality and cheerfulness." This gift is a practical gift. While all Christians should practice the discipline of giving through the minimum of 10% (tithe), God has given this gift to certain members of the body to give remarkably greater amounts of their income with liberality and great joy. These people have an acute awareness that all they have belongs to the Lord and they are merely stewards, therefore they know that God will supply their needs and richly bless them in their giving. Scriptures: Matthew 6:2-4; Mark 12:41-44; Romans 12:8; 1 Corinthians 13:3; 2 Corinthians 8:1-7; 9:2-8; Philippians 4:14-19.

Since I have the gift of giving, I can share with you some of my experience in giving. I actually love to give. It is such a wonderful feeling being able to help others by either giving to them, using monetary methods, giving information that a need or just doing something for them. The gift of giving doesn't necessarily have to always be financial. It can be the giving of your time as well. People with this gift actually don't like to be asked to give rather we want to be able to give from the heart when instructed by the Holy Spirit. One of the reasons is because giving is so rewarding to us that we will give away the shirts on our backs to make sure others have what they need. If we give away items that someone needs and we were not lead to do so, we end up giving away something that we need ourselves. After we have given it away and that feeling of fulfillment goes away, we say to ourselves; why did I give that away? I will give you a perfect example, one day my sister in law was visiting from out of town and she was looking through my closet and noticed some of my dresses and other pieces of clothing that she wanted to wear in a fashion show. As she was looking through my closet, trying some of my close on, she said to me, "you have

Spiritual Gifts

Unveiling Your Inner Light

gained weight you can't wear these dresses or these pants anymore so you should give them to me." Well, they looked very good on her and fit her well. Because she needed clothes as well, I said to her "you can keep those pieces of clothing because I don't know if I will ever get down to that size again." It felt very good being able to give her some of my clothes.

About four months later I lost 20 pounds and needless to say I didn't have any clothes that would fit me anymore. Everything was either too big or I just did not have them to wear at all. I had to go out and buy new jeans and new dresses because I gave them away before I prayed about it. I was not happy with myself and I did not have the heart to go back to her and say can I have my cloths back because she was tickled pink with the fact that she had clothes now and could not afford to buy them. I was a bit upset with myself and said if I had prayed about it first, I would not have to go out now and buy new clothes. To this day I am still trying to replace the items that I gave her out of my wardrobe. This is why it is better for us to give by our own free will without someone actually asking us to give them something, for people who have the gift of giving.

Also with this gift of giving, comes the gift of money management. We are very good at managing money in fact it is actually fun managing money. Whenever I hear people say they have to balance their checkbooks I don't quite understand that because to me what do you mean by balancing your checkbook? You know the amount of money you had in the bank, you know how much the fees are each month and you know how much you spent, what about that needs to be balanced? Not everyone has that gift. My friend always teases me and say, "Yvonne you can squeeze in nickel so tight to make the buffalo holler". That is not a bad thing and I don't consider myself as frugal, I am just aware of every dime that I spend. I am able to keep track of every penny I spend. Again not everyone can do that. So, if you find that your spouse or roommate is constantly giving away everything in the house, including furniture and they are a child of God you should have them take a spiritual gifts test to see if they have the gift of giving. You could also pray and ask God to reveal to you if they have the gift of giving and he will. If they have the gift of giving and you don't understand this gift or how they operate out of this gift, it can create serious problems in your relationship because they don't really understand why you are getting so worked up about it and you don't understand why they keep giving everything away. We look at it as even though we give it away God will replenish it for us and we are blessed by it and we are fulfilled and only operating out of our purpose. It really helps to understand the gift of giving.

Knowledge:

"The special ability to discover, accumulate, analyze, and clarify information and ideas which are pertinent to the well-being of the others." These people delights in research in order to validate the truth. Those with the gift of knowledge are at home in a book or studying. Those with this gift will often spend countless hours researching information. These people are interested in ideas and problem solving through gathering information and studying. Often, those with this gift have a low need for people. The primary method of learning with this gift is reading and studying books and other written materials. Scriptures: Luke 1:1-4; Acts 5:1-11; 1 Corinthians 2:14; 12:8; 2 Corinthians 11:6; Colossians 1:10; 2:2-3; 1 Timothy 2:15.

This is also one of my gifts. It is so very true that people with the gift of knowledge are interested in gathering information, researching and studying the information we have found because this is truly describing me. I spend a lot of my time reading, researching and trying to come up with reasons why things happen the way they do. I do a lot of problem-solving and when I solve the problem I want to validate it by showing documents of proof that what I am saying is the actual truth. People constantly come to me with their problems looking for a way to solve them. I usually start out by saying did you pray about its first before you came to me. I read many spiritual books. I read the bible a lot, pretty much daily because when people have questions about life and why they are going through what they are going through, I want to be able to validate it with the truth and the truth is in the word of God. I may not be able to quote scriptures, but I can show you where to find it in the bible and review of the scriptures to back up what I am saying to you. I will never give you advice about something without researching it first so I can tell you where I got it from and that I did not just pull it out of the sky or make it up. Whether I am researching from scriptures or scientific, health and healing, mathematical books, etc. the point is, I will validate my statements.

Leadership:

"The special ability to set goals in accordance with purpose for the future and to communicate these goals to others in such a way that they voluntarily and harmoniously work together to accomplish those goals" People with this gift are often focused on the greater goal of the group and are not overly concerned with the details. Leaders delegate tasks and details to others to accomplish the greater goal. Leaders are visionaries. Leaders have followers-a visionary without followers is not a leader. Scriptures: Luke 9:51; Acts 6:1-7; 15:7-11; Romans 12:8; 1 Timothy 5:17; Hebrews 13:17.

People with this gift are amazing to me. They had a wonderful vision of how to move forward into the future and be blessed. One of my best friends owns one of the companies I work for and she has the gift of leadership. Whenever I listen to her talk about the mission of the company and her vision for the future, I am just truly amazed of how she can think of those things off the top of her head. Her mind is constantly going. She is very good at setting goals and telling you how to reach those goals. She makes it look very easy, but trust me it is not. She came up with an idea to create this company over 20 years ago. Having a great idea and assembling a team to bring a certain concept to life is one of the first steps in creating a successful business venture. While finding a new and unique idea is rare enough; the ability to successfully execute this idea is what separates the dreamers from the entrepreneurs who have the gift of leadership. Whatever ethical plane you hold yourself to, when you are responsible for a team of people, as my friend Corliss is, it's important to raise the bar even higher. Her business and her employees are a reflection of who she is as a leader, and because she makes her honest and ethical behavior a key value, her team follows her lead.

You don't have to necessarily run a company because you have the gift of leadership. Your gift of leadership can also be utilized in the church in the community. The Holy Spirit gives the spiritual gift of leadership to some in the church to care for God's people and lead them into deeper relationship with Christ and each other. They base their success on how well they help others succeed and grow in their spiritual walk with Jesus. They are able to accomplish many different tasks and objectives as they lead, but they will always lead relationally and with a deep concern for the well-being of others. As I said before, they are visionaries! Many are entrepreneurial and willing to take risks to see the kingdom of God advanced through the church. They will go to great lengths to protect those under their care and are well-equipped to lead through crisis situations.

Teaching:

"The special ability to communicate information relevant to others in such a way that others will learn." People with the gift of teaching enjoy studying materials in order to communicate what they have learned to others Those with this gift find it easy to organize vast amounts of information in such a way as to make it easy to communicate, understand, and remember. Scriptures: Matthew 7:28-29; 28:19-20; Acts 15:32; Romans 12:6; 1 Corinthians 12:10, 28; Ephesians 4:11-14.

My mom has the gift of teaching. She taught us many things while we were growing up and loved doing it. She had this way with words explaining things so it made since. I once asked her was this something as a child that she wanted to do with she grew up. She told me yes that she always knew in her heart that she would become a teacher. Not only was she very successful teaching her students but she was just as successful teaching us at home as well. Everyone knew she had the gift. She was also the Sunday school teacher and later became the Sunday school superintendent because she was so gifted.

Her gift of teaching wasn't just teaching from a book, it was teaching us from her own personal experiences so we didn't have to go through what she went through in a particular situation. She wanted us to learn from her mistakes. Whenever I had questions about a particular subject she was always there to help me understand and show me a ways of working it out. One of the reasons I do manage money well is because of her teaching me. One day I went to her because I was troubled that all of my friends that lived in the same neighborhood had many more material things than we did and they only had one parent that worked. We on the other hand had my mother and Father working plus my Mom held down two jobs. I was really upset with the fact that we would never get new clothes from the store like other people. My Mom made all of our clothes or either we had to have hand me downs.

At Christmas we would only have one gift under the tree per person and when I would go to my friends and asked what they got for Christmas and find out not only did they get a lot of new clothes, they would have many more toys, a bike and money. Well needless to say I was really embarrassed to tell them what I got for Christmas, so I would make up things to say I got in addition to clothes. There were 5 children in my family. I asked my Mom how was that even possible that we had 3 incomes coming into the house and we were still struggling. She sat me down and said she would explain why she had to work two jobs.

My Mom took her paystub along with my dad's and placed them in front of me. She told me to add up the amount of both checks together. She then had me write down what she brought home from the second job she was working. At the time, I was thinking "ok this is good". She placed the bills on the table and said now subtract these bills from that total amount. When I subtracted the bills I was thinking "wow this is a lot". Once I did that she then said now subtract this amount for the cost of food and gas to get to work. By that time we were in the negative. She then said what you think we could do differently.

I asked her why the neighbors and other relatives got more things when they don't even make as much money as we do. She then explain about some of them take out loans to buy gifts and take all year to pay it off and others are doing illegal things in order to bring more money in the house and both of those were unacceptable in our family. Well of course I was lost for words and said I was glad that she shared that with me and I now understood. I never got upset again. That was just one situation but there were many more that she was able to teach me in a way that it stuck with me all of my life and helped me as I went through things when I was older.

Spiritual Gifts _____
Unveiling Your Inner Light

Wisdom:

The special ability to know how given knowledge may best be applied to specific needs. Those with this gift have an excellent ability to apply truth to everyday life. Often, people in the church naturally seek out people with this gift when they are facing complicated spiritual problems. When a person with this gift considers past experience, they realize that they often make good and correct decisions and judgments. Scriptures: Proverbs 4:5-8; Acts 6:3, 10; 15:13-20; 20:20-21; Romans 12:17; 1 Corinthians 12:28; Ephesians 4:11-14; Colossians 1:28.

My Mom and grandmother had this gift. Many people may receive information and gifts from the Holy Spirit, but do not always know how to deliver, nor to whom. When we do not minister in God's wisdom we can make mistakes and even show insensitivity to the person or people we are delivering the information to, which can often cause offence. The gift may be right, but the manner of which you deliver it may be wrong. My Mom had a way of delivering information to us that not only was accepted in love, but made sense and it was easy to apply the information she gave to a particular situation that made it better than what my initial understanding was.

The people who have the gift of wisdom often have an ability to synthesize biblical truth and apply it to people's lives so that they make good choices and avoid foolish mistakes. The people with this gift also can function well as coaches, counselors, and consultants. This gift describes someone who can understand and speak forth biblical truth in such a way as to skillfully apply it to life situations with all discernment.

Mercy:

"The special ability that God gives to certain members of the Body of Christ to feel genuine empathy and compassion for individuals (both Christian and non-Christian) who suffer from distressing physical, mental, or emotional problems, and to translate that compassion into cheerfully done deeds which reflect Christ's love and alleviate the suffering." This gift is a practical gift. Those with this gift find themselves visiting and assisting those in need, and often feel the pain of the person they are helping within themselves. People with this gift find it extremely difficult not to help those who seem less fortunate than themselves. Those with this gift generally enjoy helping those with physical or mental problems and do well in ministries involving visiting hospitals, nursing homes, prisons, and shut-ins. Scriptures: Matthew 20:29-34; 25:24-40; Mark 9:41; Luke 10:33-35; Acts 11:28-30; 16:33-34; Romans 12:8; Jude 22-23.

Note: The gifts of Helps, Mercy, and Service are often confused. Helps focuses on Christian works and freeing others to accomplish their God-given ministries. Mercy focuses on people in distress and reflects God's love and compassion. Service focuses on accomplishing little tasks that may otherwise go undone in order to move the greater goal of the ministry or church toward completion.

Mercy is a gift that you really have to be careful with. Sometimes if people know you have this gift they will try to take advantage of your compassion toward people who are in need. They know what buttons to push in order to get you to help them whether you should or shouldn't. For example, I have a friend you owns a company and because it is a small company, she wears many hats.

There may be a situation where she needs to fire someone and she has a very hard time doing that, even though it is detrimental to future of her company. She sometimes confides in me what is happening with some of her employees and the challenges she has. After listening to her complaint, I will say to her that person needs to be terminated because this will affect the company's accreditation and if we don't get recertified that will be a major problem for the future of this company. Even though she knows what I am saying is true, she will say ok I will fire him next week.

The next week will come and he is still there. I asked her what happened and why is he still with the company and her response is "it was a holiday, I can't fire someone around a holiday, and I will do it next week". A month will go pass and I will ask her about that same person and then her response was "his wife has the flu, I can't fire him with his wife being sick". My point is she procrastinates because of her compassion for people and showing mercy because of their circumstances.

Healing:

The special ability that God gives to certain members of the Body of Christ to serve as human intermediaries through whom God cures illness and restores health apart from the use of natural means. This gift is a sign gift. Many attribute the occurrence of supernatural healing to a certain level of faith. Those who have this gift must use it knowing that the healing only occurs within the limits of God's will, and therefore miraculous healing will not always occur. Those with this gift must also recognize that God does often choose to use medical science to bring about healing in a person; therefore doctors and medicine are not obsolete. Miraculous healing will only occur if it will bring the greatest glory to God and effectively grow His church. Scriptures: Acts 3:1-10; 5:12-16; 9:32-35; 28:7-10; 1 Corinthians 12:9, 28.

Note on Healing and Miracles: The gifts of healing and miracles are often combined, since they both involve the occurrence of events beyond natural means. However, one is focused on the healing of the human body, while the other is focused on other miraculous events that alter the ordinary course of nature. These may in fact be two separate manifestations of the same gift.

My experience with healing happened when I was a teenager and didn't understand the different gifts at the time. All I know is my sister was always sick because she was allergic to so many things like pollen, plants, animals, different foods etc… She had the worst case of Eczema that the doctors at that time had ever seen. She was constantly in and out of the hospital because of it. Her skin would be so bad that it looked like an alligator's skin. When she would stretch out her arm or leg the skin would sometimes crack and bleed. They would have to put her in the hospital on steroids for weeks at a time. One day my Aunt Betty who had the gift of healing called my Mother and asked her to send my sister to her home to stay with her for the summer and she would heal her and she didn't need to continue to go to the hospital because the doctors were not doing anything for her.

My Mother said at that point she would try anything. The drove my sister to my Aunt's house which was a 12 hour drive from where we lived at the time. Three months later my parents brought her back and we were all amazed at the beauty of her skin. Not only was her skin as soft as a baby's skin there were no spots or scars anywhere on her body. My Mom said when she asked my Aunt what she did to get her skin looking so good she said" I laid my hands on her body and prayed for her daily and fed her a nutritional diet with no junk food and lots of fruits and vegetables and I could see she was feeling better and her skin was healing nicely". I also had experience with my Aunt healing me as well.

When I was about 12 years old, I once had stomach pains so bad that I could not move. My Mom was debating whether or not to take me to the hospital and my Aunt Betty happened to be visiting us at the time. My Aunt said to my Mom "let me pray for her first before you take her to the hospital". My Aunt laid her hands on my stomach and I could feel her hands getting very hot has she prayed. Well needless to say that pain immediately went away and we were all surprised. All my Mom said was thank you Jesus! At that time I didn't know anything about spiritual gifts, I was just so happy that the pain in my stomach went away. Now when I look back on that situation, I know my Aunt had the gift of healing.

Interpretation of Tongues:

"The special ability that God gives to certain members of the Body of Christ to make known in the vernacular the message of one who speaks in tongues." This gift is a sign gift. Those with this gift are used to bring the personal edification of tongues to a position where the message edifies the group in which the tongue was spoken. Those with this gift gain a sense of what God is trying to say when they hear a person speak in tongues. Should a person with this gift fail to interpret the tongue when it is spoken and they receive the interpretation through the Holy Spirit, they have done a great disservice to the person who spoke in tongues and to the group as the edification that God desires has not taken place. Often, the interpreter is also the person who has spoken in tongues. The interpretation of tongues is often closely related to the message given by an exhorter or a prophet. Scriptures: 1 Corinthians 12:10-30; 14:13-17, 26-28.

Spiritual Gifts _____

Unveiling Your Inner Light

Note on Tongues and Interpretation of Tongues: When used in a group setting, an interpretation must take place, or else the one speaking the tongue should remain silent. If a tongue is spoken without an interpretation, the speaker is edified. If the tongue is interpreted, it is for the edification of the body.

Miracles:

The special ability that God gives to certain members of the Body of Christ to serve as human intermediaries through whom God performs powerful acts that are perceived by observers to have altered the ordinary course of nature. This gift is a sign gift. This gift is manifested through the supernatural intervention by God into specific circumstances in order to change the perceived natural outcome. Those with this gift must recognize that God only causes miracles to happen in order to bring the greatest glory to himself. Scriptures: Acts 9:36-42; 19:11-20; 20:7-12; Romans 15:17-19; 1 Corinthians 1:22-25; 12:10, 28; 2 Corinthians 12:12.

Note on Healing and Miracles: The gifts of healing and miracles are often combined, since they both involve the occurrence of events beyond natural means. However, one is focused on the healing of the human body, while the other is focused on other miraculous events that alter the ordinary course of nature. These may in fact be two separate manifestations of the same gift.

Prophecy:

The special ability that God gives to certain members of the Body of Christ to receive and communicate an immediate message of God to His people with authority and urgency perceived by the hearers. This gift is a communication gift. Those with the gift of prophecy will often feel as though they have a direct word from God that will comfort, encourage, guide, warn, or rebuke the Body of Christ. Prophets are concerned about evangelism and will have a desire speak strongly against evil in society or in the church. Prophets have a great sense of urgency to their message. Unless paired with the gifts of exhortation or teaching, prophets will often not feel the need to explain their message, but will expect immediate response. The message of a prophet must always be tested in line with Scripture. Prophets would be wise to test their message against Scripture prior to delivering the message, and using Scriptural precedent in delivery of their message. Scriptures: Luke 7:26; Acts 15:32; 21:9-11; Romans 12:6; 1 Corinthians 12:10, 28; 14:3, 24-25, 29, 36-38; Ephesians 4:11-14.

Note: Exhortation, Prophecy, and Teaching are considered the communication gifts. The distinctions for each gift are often confused. Often, gifted communicators have a mix of these gifts. Exhortation focuses on personal and practical application of the message or truth being communicated. Prophecy focuses purely on the message or truth to be communicated. Teaching focuses on bringing thorough or adequate understanding of the message or truth being communicated.

I know of 3 people my life that has been blessed with the gift of prophecy. One of them was a minister of music at the church I was attending when I lived in California. My husband and I had a house built and with my gift of discernment I always have ministers or Pastor Come to any place I moved to in order to bless the house or apartment, rebuking any spirit that is not of God. Well not only did Tony have the gift of Prophecy he also has the gift of discernment.

It was his discerning spirit I wanted just to have confirmation that there were no bad spirits in that house we moved in. Well needless to say Tony blessed the house with oil and prayed for us. As he walked around the with Joy because he was so happy that we bought the house as we were not sure if we would even qualify for that particular house, Tony said " I bet you are wondering why God blessed you with this 5 bedroom house". Well I was actually thinking to myself "no I am just happy that he did". I then said, well I guess I am just to see where he was going with this. Tony went on to say" He blessed you with this house because your two step sons will be coming out to California from Wisconsin to live with you now".

I told him that was impossible because we were in such a long court battle with my husband's ex-wife concerning the boys even to get visitation rights. He then went on to say "trust me I know what God just told me". I then went on to say" I know you have the gift of Prophecy but we are all human and I just don't believe that will ever happen". Tony said well you need to believe this because it is going to happen. He then went on to say "in fact it will happen before the end of this year" which was in 4 months. I told him again, "That can't be because his Ex-wife told me that she will die before she would ever let those boys come and live with us". He then said with assurance "I know what the spirit just told me and I guess those boys will be going to her funeral because they will be permanently living with you before the end of this year". I was shocked that he said that and didn't say another word but okay.

Months went by and I completely forgot I even had that conversation with Tony. One evening we received a phone call from my husband's ex-wife and all she said was "the boys are coming to live with you and you won". My husband and I were both shocked and said that we didn't believe her and questioned her motives. We then went and retained an attorney and told him the situation and drew up papers and she signed them without hesitation. We didn't understand what was happening. After the boys were with us for a year, what Tony said came to my mind and I was overwhelmed and speechless. I then reminded my husband of what he said and he was overwhelmed as well. He said, "I completely forgot about that conversation." All we could say was thank you Jesus for bring that back to our remembrance. Now we are able to share that situation with a wonderful testimony to other people to show them how God can turn a bad situation into good one pretty much overnight.

Service:

"The special ability that God gives to certain members of the Body of Christ to identify the unmet needs involved in a task related to God's work, and to make use of available resources to meet those needs and help accomplish the desired results." This gift is a practical gift. Those with the gift of service enjoy doing routine tasks around the church regardless of how they affect others. Those with this gift enjoy menial tasks and do them cheerfully. Service-oriented people would rather take orders than give them. Scriptures: John 12:26; Acts 6:1-7; Romans 12:6-7; Galatians 6:2, 9-10; 2 Timothy 1:16-18; Titus 3:14.

Note: The gifts of Helps, Mercy, and Service are often confused. Helps focuses on Christian works and freeing others to accomplish their God-given ministries. Mercy focuses on people in distress and reflects God's love and compassion. Service focuses on accomplishing little tasks that may otherwise go undone in order to move the greater goal of the ministry or church toward completion.

I know several people with this gift. My sister Kay, my Aunt Jerlene who is constantly running errands and cooking for other people, my niece Tiffany who is always running errands and taking care of other people's kids. People with this gift will tire you out by just watching them operate out of their gift. They love what they are doing and do it cheerfully. My sister Kay never seems to sit down and rest until she is ready to drop. She is constantly running errands, driving here and there, doing things for other people like organizing events, putting together party favors, helping people fill out their taxes, putting together fund raisers for the church, etc.. And she is as happy as a bee doing it.

When I watch her I get tired and will ask her to please sit down somewhere. She just looks at me and laughs and says "I'm ok, I don't mind doing this". I just can't imagine having this gift! I know that if I did have this gift it would have been what God wanted me to have and he would equip me so I would not get tired like my sister, Aunt and niece.

Tongues:

"The special ability that God gives to certain members of the Body of Christ (a) to speak to God in a language that they have never learned and/or (b) to receive and communicate a message of God to his people through a divinely anointed utterance in a language they never learned. "This gift is a sign gift. Tongues is often associated with intercession and/or faith, but must be recognized as not necessarily being the sign of the baptism of the Holy Spirit or even as evidence of the filling of the Holy Spirit. Tongues, like any other spiritual gift, is given by God to whomever He chooses to be used to His glory and the edification of the Church. 1 Corinthians 13:1 suggests that there are two forms of the gift of tongues: tongues of men and tongues of angels. This would mean that the speaker could be speaking in an earthly language, or in a language beyond normal human understanding. Scriptures: Mark 16:17; Acts 2:1-13; 10:44-46; 19:1-7; Romans 8:26-27; 1 Corinthians 12:10,28; 13:1; 14:13-19, 26-28, 39.

Note on Tongues and Interpretation of Tongues: When used in a group setting, an interpretation must take place, or else the one speaking the tongue should remain silent. If a tongue is spoken without an interpretation, the speaker is edified. If the tongue is interpreted, it is for the edification of the body.

Apostleship:

In the bible, persons with the gift of apostleship are missionaries. A missionary is one who lives as Jesus did, as a missional itinerant. Persons with the gift of apostleship are able to minister in a second culture. They give effective leadership in new places for the purpose of teaching the gospel, starting new congregations, and training and enabling leaders. They work to extend God's realm of justice. Second Corinthians 12:12 reminds us that they are persons of outstanding patience. However as we read in 1 Corinthians 4:8-13, the gift of apostleship is not without cost: apostles are spectacles to the world, fools for the sake of Christ, and are hungry, poorly clothed, and held in disrepute. Scriptures: 2 Peter 1:21; 2 Timothy 3:16 Titus 1:5; Acts 20:28 ; Acts 14:23; Acts 2:1-47; Matthew 28:19.

Evangelism:

The gift of evangelism is the ability and desire to boldly and clearly communicate the gospel of Jesus Christ so that non-Christians can become Christians. Evangelists often care passionately about lost people and have a strong desire to see them meet Jesus. They feel compassion for the lost and seek to earnestly understand their questions and doubts so that they can provide a compelling answer. An evangelist often prefers being with people in the culture rather than hanging out with Christians in the church. Scriptures: Mark 16:15; Matthew 28:19-20; 1 Corinthians 9:22; Matthew 9:37-38; Isaiah 6:8; Acts 1:8

Pastoring:

The Greek word "poimen" means pastor. In Paul's spiritual gifts listing in Ephesians 4:11, this term is translated "pastor." Although the word "poimen" is translated pastor only one time in Scripture it is used sixteen additional times. The remaining sixteen are all translated "shepherd." Therefore, we are actually discussing the GIFT of shepherding, not the POSITION of pastor. Though a good pastor must have the gift of shepherding, everyone who has the gift of shepherding is not called to be pastor. The gift can be used in many positions in a church.

As a gifted shepherd, you have the Spirit-given capacity and desire to serve God by overseeing, training, and caring for the needs of a group of Christians. You are usually very patient, people-centered, and willing to spend time in prayer for others. You tend to be a "Jack of All and Master of ONE," meaning you are usually dominant in one of the speaking gifts (evangelist, prophet, teacher, exhorter) as well. You are often authoritative, more a leader than a follower, and expressive, composed, and sensitive. Your pleasing personality draws people to you.

You have a burden to see others learn and grow and are protective of those under your care. You want to present the whole Word of God and do not like to present the same materials more than once. You are willing to study what is necessary to feed your group and are more relationship oriented than task oriented. You are a peace-maker and diplomat-very tolerant of people's weaknesses. You tend to remember people's names and faces. You are more concerned with doing for others than others doing for you. You are faithful and devoted and may become a workaholic. You can become an all-purpose person in order to meet needs. Scriptures: Acts 6:1-7; Jeremiah 3:15; 1 Peter 5:1-14; 1 Peter 2:1-25; Titus 2:1; James 3:1; 1 Timothy 3:1-7; Ephesians 4:11; 1 Timothy 3:2; Ephesians 4:1-32; 1 Peter 2:5; 1 Timothy 3:1.

CHAPTER 4
Places To Use Your Spiritual Gifts

Exhortation/Encouragement:

Coming alongside someone with words of comfort and counsel to build them up (Rom. 12:8).

Examples of ministries that use this gift:

Prayer rooms, Special Needs, hospital visitation, employment transition, men's and women's small group facilitator, care groups for those in marriage, divorce, infertility, job loss, or with cancer.

Evangelism:

Joyfully and courageously sharing the message of the Gospel (Eph. 4:11).

Examples of ministries that use this gift:

Prayer rooms, summer sport camps, mission trips, community outreach events.

Faith:

Conviction and confidence in God's ability to accomplish His purpose irrespective of circumstances (1 Cor. 12:8-10).

Examples of ministries that use this gift:

Mentoring, mission trips, community outreach, care groups for those in marriage, divorce, infertility, job loss, or with cancer, prayer rooms.

Spiritual Gifts

Unveiling Your Inner Light

Giving:

Joyfully and generously sharing one's money and possessions without expecting repayment (Rom. 12:8).

Examples of ministries that use this gift:

Drives for school supplies, clothing, and food, fundraising projects, debt elimination projects, benevolence teams, Thanksgiving and Christmas gift projects.

Service:

Assisting others so they are free to minister (Rom. 12:7, 1 Cor. 12:28, Eph. 4:12).

Examples of ministries that use this gift:

Sunday morning guest services, ushers, and parking lot teams, hospitality teams, office volunteers, service teams with children, students, or adults.

Leadership:

Communicating ministry direction and motivating others to accomplish it, all from a servant's heart (Rom. 12:8).

Examples of ministries that use this gift:

Elder team, small group or class leader, special event leader (these areas are hand-selected by pastoral staff from out of existing volunteers who demonstrate servant-heartedness, teachability, and leadership ability or potential).

Mercy:

Sensing someone's need and providing relief (Rom. 12:8).

Examples of ministries that use this gift:

Hospital visitation, benevolence teams, special needs, community care events, prayer rooms.

Pastoring:

Nurturing and guiding others in their spiritual growth (Eph. 4:11).

Examples of ministries that use this gift:

Lead and care for a small group with children, students, or adults in things like discipleship, Bible study, financial study, marriage, divorce, infertility, and cancer care groups, Sunday morning and weeknight fellowship groups and classes.

Teaching:

Explaining the Bible in an understandable way that leads to application ad

growth (Rom. 12:7, 1 Cor. 12:28, Eph. 4:11).

Examples of ministries that use this gift:

Mission trips, Sunday morning and weeknight fellowship groups and classes for children, students or adults, teacher for special events with children, students, or adults, teacher for financial study, or a care group for those married/divorced/infertile/with cancer.

CHAPTER 5
What is my Purpose

If we do not know our real purpose in life; our reason for existing, life is very meaningless indeed. Yet, God created each of us with a special purpose in mind. There is something that needs to be done on this earth that can only be done by you. Many people go through life feeling discouraged about themselves and thinking they do not have a purpose in life. However that's not true. Whoever you are——whatever your life experiences, talents, physical ability, or role——you have a purpose. God created you. You are not an accident. God has a plan for you.

While it's true some people seem to find their life purpose easier than others, it's also true that God really does have a plan for every single person, even if it takes a while to see what it is. Don't focus on how long it is taking. You're not alone. There are lots of people in your shoes. Take a look at the disciples. Now, there's a diverse group. Before Jesus came on the scene, they were fishermen, tax collectors, farmers, etc. They must have been good at what they were doing because they were feeding their families and making a living.

But then they met Jesus, and their true callings came into focus very quickly. What the disciples didn't know was that God wanted them to be happy—even more than they did. And following God's plan for their lives made them happy inside, where it really mattered.

Purpose is perhaps one of the deepest human longings. Many famous people have reached the top of his or her field and declared the success to be meaningless. There is a deeper need that success just doesn't seem to fill. Philosophers and psychologists have tried to tackle the looming question of purpose – largely without completely satisfying answers. Countless dollars are spent on our search for purpose in life. We try to squeeze meaning out of any and every pursuit. So is there purpose in this life?

Spiritual Gifts _____
Unveiling Your Inner Light

You were made by God and you were made for God, and until you understand that, life isn't going to make sense. When you come to this question, what is my purpose, you only have three alternatives.

1. First, I will use the mystical approach, and that is look within. You find this in a lot of talk shows, a lot of new age books and a lot of seminars. They say, "look within to discover your purpose." The only problem is that doesn't work. We've all looked within and didn't like what we saw. It's quite confusing. In fact, if you could know the purpose of your life by looking within, we'd all know it by now. Looking within doesn't work.

2. Let's look at a second way you can try to discover your purpose and that is called the intellectual or philosophical approach. That's where you go to a seminary or university class and ask questions like, "Why am I here? Where did I come from? Where am I going?" What is the meaning and purpose of life?" Once you have read several books from well-known novelists, scientists, intellectuals, and after attending classes, it can be quite depressing because you still end up asking the question "If you know the purpose, can you please tell me?"

3. Please understand that there's a better answer to speculation and that's revelation. If I were to show you an invention that you have never seen before, you wouldn't know its purpose. The only way you'd know its purpose was either talk to the inventor, the creator who made it or read the owner's manual. The owner's manual of life is the bible and your Creator is God. It is only as you get to know God that you will discover his purposes for your life. If finding your life purpose seems like an elusive undertaking, don't panic! You are not alone. I hope you'll begin that journey today.

"For we are God's workmanship, created in Christ Jesus to do good works, which God prepared in advance for us to do" (Ephesians 2:1).

- One purpose in life is to glorify God in this world.

- One purpose in life is to praise and worship God.

- One purpose in life is to grow in character.

Spiritual Gifts _____

Unveiling Your Inner Light

- One purpose in life is to tell others about Jesus' love for them.
- One purpose in life is to develop your spiritual gifts.

Just as each of us has one body with many members, and these members do not all have the same function, so in Christ we who are many form one body, and each member belongs to all the others. We have different gifts, according to the grace given us. If a man's gift is prophesying, let him use it in proportion to his faith. If it is serving, let him serve; if it is teaching, let him teach; if it is encouraging, let him encourage; if it is contributing to the needs of others, let him give generously; if it is leadership, let him govern diligently; if it is showing mercy, let him do it cheerfully (Romans 12:4-8).

Finding purpose in life is perhaps the greatest human quest. It is a theme in any stage of life, largely because our specific purposes may change – or at least be carried out differently – in different seasons of life. Thankfully, believers can rest in the fact that their lives do have purpose. God created us with intent, He knows His plans for us (Jeremiah 29:11; Ephesians 2:10), and He is eager to reveal Himself to us. He desires that we know Him, that we enjoy Him, that we witness about Him, and that we live out our unique role in His Body.

The type of person you become is more important than your successes and failures in the world. But the fruit of the Spirit is love, joy, peace, patience, kindness, goodness, faithfulness, gentleness and self-control (Galatians 5:22-23). Life has definite meaning and definite purpose. The Holy Bible is our source for everything pertaining to life and godliness as described in 2 Peter 1:3.

Ephesians 2:10 says, "For we are his workmanship, created in Christ Jesus for good works, which God prepared beforehand, that we should walk in them." There are universal good works prepared for us – such as obedience to Christ, witnessing, and enjoying God – but there are also individual works. The Bible is replete with examples of God's personal touch on people's lives. The prophets were individually called by God for a specific time and purpose. Abraham, Noah, Joseph, Ruth, Esther, Mary, and multiple others were used of God in their times, with their abilities, and for His purposes. First Corinthians 12:12-31 talks about the Church in terms of a body. Each member of the Church has a different purpose, just as each portion of the body is used for different things. Romans 12:6-8 and 1 Corinthians 12:4-11 list several spiritual gifts a person might have. We know from science and psychology that people are unique. No one in the world is exactly like you. God made that design. Psalm 139 is a beautiful depiction of the care with which God created us. He "knitted [us] together in [our] mother[s]'s womb[s]" (Psalm 139:13b). There is a unique purpose that God has just for you.

So how do we discover the purpose of our lives? There are many tools that Christians use, including personality tests, spiritual gifts tests, recitation of life history with an eye toward life themes, and the like. Perhaps the best tool is simply to pray. We can ask God to reveal His purpose for our lives. When we do so, we need to listen to what He says. We should examine Scripture to confirm that what we think we hear God saying is, in fact, biblical. We should also look at various events in our lives, pay attention to our strengths, and pay attention to outside wisdom (Proverbs 15:22; Proverbs 12:15). God will not direct us to do something contrary to His character or His word.

Purpose Scriptures

Jeremiah 29:11

For I know the plans I have for you, declares the Lord, plans for welfare and not for evil, to give you a future and a hope.

Romans 8:28

And we know that for those who love God all things work together for good, for those who are called according to his purpose.

Ephesians 3:8-12

To me, though I am the very least of all the saints, this grace was given, to preach to the Gentiles the unsearchable riches of Christ, and to bring to light for everyone what is the plan of the mystery hidden for ages in God who created all things, so that through the church the manifold wisdom of God might now be made known to the rulers and authorities in the heavenly places. This was according to the eternal purpose that he has realized in Christ Jesus our Lord, in whom we have boldness and access with confidence through our faith in him.

1 Corinthians 6:19-20

Or do you not know that your body is a temple of the Holy Spirit within you, whom you have from God? You are not your own, for you were bought with a price. So glorify God in your body.

Acts 22:16

And now why do you wait? Rise and be baptized and wash away your sins, calling on his name.'

Mark 16:16

Whoever believes and is baptized will be saved, but whoever does not believe will be condemned.

Ephesians 1:11

In him we have obtained an inheritance, having been predestined according to the purpose of him who works all things according to the counsel of his will.

2 Corinthians 12:9

But he said to me, "My grace is sufficient for you, for my power is made perfect in weakness." Therefore I will boast all the more gladly of my weaknesses, so that the power of Christ may rest upon me.

Proverbs 22:6

Train up a child in the way he should go; even when he is old he will not depart from it.

Psalm 20:4

May he grant you your heart's desire and fulfill all your plans!

Mark 16:15-16

And he said to them, "Go into all the world and proclaim the gospel to the whole creation. Whoever believes and is baptized will be saved, but whoever does not believe will be condemned.

Proverbs 1:1-7

The proverbs of Solomon, son of David, king of Israel: To know wisdom and instruction, to understand words of insight, to receive instruction in wise dealing, in righteousness, justice, and equity; to give prudence to the simple, knowledge and discretion to the youth— Let the wise hear and increase in learning, and the one who understands obtain guidance, ...

CHAPTER 6
What are the Some Basic Life Principles?

Design, Authority, Responsibility, Suffering, Ownership, Freedom, Success

Just as there are universal laws that govern the world of nature, there are basic principles that govern our personal lives and relationships as Disciples of Christ. These seven Biblical principles apply to every person, regardless of culture, background, religion, age, education, or social status. An understanding of these principles can bring insights into the cause-and-effect sequences of life. Consequently, individuals can become equipped to make wise choices and avoid failure.

Design

God has a precise purpose for each person, object, and relationship that He creates. As we understand and live in harmony with His design, we will discover self-acceptance, identity, and fulfillment in life.

Authority

God assigns various responsibilities to parents, church leaders, government officials, and other authorities. As we learn to acknowledge and honor these authorities, we can see God work through them to provide direction and protection in our lives. Honoring our authorities brings inward peace.

Responsibility

God holds us accountable for every word, thought, action, attitude, and motive. When we offend others, asking for forgiveness and making proper restitution are essential steps to maintaining a clear conscience.

Unveiling Your Inner Light

Suffering

The hurts of offenders can reveal our "blind spots." God grants us grace for personal cleansing, growth, and achievement as we learn to respond with full forgiveness to those who offend us.

Ownership

Everything we have has been entrusted to us by God, and we are to use these resources wisely. Yielding our personal rights and expectations to God brings true security and enables us to overcome anger and worry.

Freedom

Godly freedom is not the privilege to do what we want; rather, Godly freedom is the power to do what is right. Regaining ground that has been surrendered to sin brings moral purity, equipping us to serve others in genuine love.

Success

We can discover God's purpose for our lives by engrafting Scripture into our hearts and minds, using it to "think God's thoughts" and to build a foundation for making wise decisions.

CHAPTER 7
Good versus Evil

If God exists, why is there evil in the world? You know, this is a difficult stumbling block and question for many people. The simplest way to look at this question is to examine God's nature and his desire for mankind. Look at the logic. God loves us and wants us to love him back. And how could we love him back unless we have the freedom to not love?

God could have made us like robots who do nothing more than say, "I love you. I love you. I love you." But, it would be forced love, not real love. Love is a choice. And if you have a choice, you have to be able to choose not to love and that in itself is the nature of evil. Evil is choosing not to love. So, when God gave us the freedom to choose, he gave us not only our greatest blessing, but he also gave us our greatest curse because we can choose to do right or choose to do wrong.

"Who did Jesus think he was? And why should I care?"

The reason there's evil in the world is not because of God, but because God gave us the freedom to choose. Now the potential for love outweighs the existence of evil, because, evil is only going to exist for a short time, but love is going last forever. All of the suffering and all of the death that we see in the world today are the result, of man choosing to make wrong choices.

God could have taken our freedom, but He didn't. I hope you'll use your freedom to choose God.

Is Jesus really God?

Well, when you think about it, you only have three options as to who Jesus Christ was. You see, Jesus claimed to be God. He said things like, "I am the way, the truth and the life. No one comes to the Father except

Spiritual Gifts

Unveiling Your Inner Light

through me." He claimed to be God many, many times. Now, that means either:

    1. He is who he says He was

    2. He was the biggest liar in history or

    3. He was crazy. He was a lunatic on the order of the man who calls himself a fried potato.

You see, you can't just say Jesus was a good man. I've had many friends who said, "Oh, I believe Jesus was a good man." Well He couldn't have been a good man and said those things He said. For instance, if I said to you, "I'm Yvonne Allen and I'm a good teacher and a good wife." You might say, "Okay, I buy that." But if I said to you, "I'm Yvonne Allen and I'm God and I'm the only way to heaven." Well, you would have to make a decision. You couldn't say I was a good person because a good person wouldn't say that. You'd either say, "She is who she says she was, or she's a liar or she's crazy."

Jesus didn't just expect us to believe Him and take Him at His word. He said, "I'm going to prove the claim that I am God." He said, "I'm going to let people kill me on a cross, then let them bury me. I'll be dead for three days and then I'll come back to life." And, of course, that was the event that changed history; the resurrection of Jesus Christ. Every person since then whether they believe in Him or not, every time you right a date, A.D. or B.C., refers to Jesus Christ. It was the event that split history when Jesus proved that He was who He said He was, He is God.

Do all religions lead to God?

Think about the logic of this. Can I go into a phone booth and dial any phone number and get home? No, there's only one number that'll get me home. I could be sincere, but I could be sincerely wrong. The truth is, all numbers don't lead to home and all roads and all religions don't lead to Christ. It all depends on which direction you take. Jesus said this, "I am the way and the truth and the light. No one comes to the Father except through me." I'm betting my life on the fact that He was right because I figured

Spiritual Gifts _____

Unveiling Your Inner Light

Jesus knows more about it than I did.

The Bible tells us that on the road to heaven, there are only two directions, toward Christ or away from Him. You can accept it or you can reject it; that's your choice. You can make Jesus the Lord of your life, the person in charge of your life, or you can call Him a liar, but that's what the Bible declares.

A lot of people sincerely believe that even though they've broken God's rules they can earn God's forgiveness by doing good works, by observing the Five Pillars of Islam or the Buddhist Eightfold Path or the Hindu Doctrine of Karma, for example. But I don't get it. How will doing some good works that we should have done all our lives, make up for all the countless times we failed? You see, Heaven is a perfect place and that means only perfect people get to go there. If imperfect people were allowed in, it wouldn't be perfect anymore. Well I don't know about you, but I stopped being perfect a long time ago. So God came up with "plan B". He came to earth in human form, Jesus Christ, and He lived a perfect life and now He offers to let us go to heaven on His ticket. I pray that you will trust Jesus Christ and stop trying to bat a thousand; you stopped doing that a long time ago. Accept God's free ticket through Jesus Christ.

What's going to happen to those people in the world who've never heard about Jesus Christ?

You may have heard this question put another way: "What about the person living in the jungle somewhere who's never heard the good news about Jesus Christ? Are you Christians saying that a person won't go to heaven based solely on where he lives?" No, we're not saying that. The Bible tells us that God doesn't work that way. We understand that God is perfect in His love and perfect in His holiness and He's perfectly just and fair. Therefore, it's against God's nature to be unfair. It's against God's nature to hide the ball on salvation or to condemn somebody who's ignorant of his truth. In fact, the bible declares that God is loving and patient and not willing that anybody should perish. But, He wants everybody to come to repentance, to come to know Him and have a relationship with him.

So if God is a perfectly loving and righteous God, then He will figure out ways to help people understand Him? He somehow reveals the simple truth of the gospel to people throughout the world. I've talked to missionaries in Africa who've told me that Jesus has revealed Himself through nature. When you look at nature you learn that God is organized, that God is creative, that God likes variety. But it's when we look at Jesus Christ we realize that God is loving.

As Christians, we are called to tell the good news to other people. It's God's decision to decide what happens to people who haven't heard about Him. But, it is our decision to take that news to as many people as possible. And the bible says we will be held more responsible because we have heard and we have known that God is love, that God wants a relationship with us and that God will forgive us if we give our lives to Jesus Christ.

So, what do we do about those who haven't heard? We tell them. First, we accept God's good news and then we tell them and we leave the result in the hands of a fair, loving and just God.

What about all the wars that are caused in the name of Christianity?

Well first, let me say that a lot of things have been done in the name of Christianity that Jesus Christ would totally disavow. And just because someone claims to be a Christian doesn't necessarily make him or her a follower of Christ, nor does it make him a representative of Jesus. It's very, very important to distinguish between the bible kind of Christianity and the actions that have been taken throughout history by people who claim to be Christians but really didn't know.

You see, there's a difference between religion and a relationship with God. Jesus is not interested in the religion of Christianity. He's interested in you having a relationship with Him. Jesus never said, "I've come that you might have religion." He said, "I came that you might have life and have it more abundantly."

Many people have claimed to be followers of Christ, but they've lived their lives contrary to His teaching. We shouldn't label that group Christian. But let me say this, have you ever seen a counterfeit dollar? Well, maybe you haven't, but maybe you've heard of them. Why are there counterfeit dollars in the world? Well, I'll tell you why. Because there are real dollars in the world. If there were no real dollars, there would be no counterfeits. And if you find counterfeit Christianity in the world, it must mean that, somewhere, there must be the real thing. The point is, we don't identify Jesus by claiming that all the things that were done in His name were done by Him. In fact, Jesus prevented His own disciples from defending themselves against the enemies when He said on a personal basis "I want you to turn the other cheek."

Numerous wars have been done in the name of Christianity that Jesus probably would have disavowed. The real issue is, do you know Jesus Christ? It doesn't matter so much what has been done by hypocrites or phonies or false followers of Christ. What matters is that you know the real, true, genuine item. Have you ever turned your life over to Jesus Christ? If you haven't, I would encourage you to investigate Him today.

Is there any real right or wrong?

You might have heard somebody say, "I don't believe there's such a thing as right or wrong." Or maybe you've heard a professor say, "There are no absolutes." Whenever I hear that I want to say, "Are you absolutely sure?" You have to ask yourself, "Is this statement even logical? Is there any right or wrong?" Because when people say, "There is no right or wrong, or it's wrong for you to impose your morals on me," think about it. By them telling you that, they are imposing their morals on you.

The fact is we all inheritantly know right from wrong and we just have this weird tendency to disregard it; to disregard morality when it conflicts with our desires for pleasure or personal gain. Now, sure, you might justify having an affair, but certainly you wouldn't condone your spouse having one. Or you might justify taking something without permission, but if you were the one being robbed you wouldn't think it was okay. There isn't a person alive today who'd come home from work and discover that their entire house had been robbed and say, "Oh, how wonderful that this burglar is able to enjoy all my things without my permission. And who am I to impose my view of right or wrong on this poor burglar?" Do you see how ridiculous that is? Of course.

Even those who claim there is no right or wrong have their own moral conscious, they've just set their own standards. Here's a good way to determine right from wrong. Turn the situation around on yourself. Jesus said it best. He said, "Treat people the same way you want people to treat you." We all know that murder, rape, lying, stealing, torture and injustice are absolutely wrong. Why? Because we wouldn't want any of these things to happen to us. The person who would say, "there is no right or wrong," would not agree that it was okay for them to be raped. No, when you turn it on yourself, you realize that even inside ourselves, God has placed a moral conscious and that conscious tells us when we do right and when we do wrong. And when we violate our conscious, we need forgiveness. That's why the bible said, "God sent Jesus to earth so that we might be forgiven of all of our wrong."

Why do I exist?

That's the most fundamental question of life. What on earth am I here for?

Well, you need to understand God to answer that question. The bible says, "God is love." It doesn't say He has love, it says He is love. It's part of His nature, His character, it is the essence of His being. God is love. Now, love isn't very valuable unless you bestow it on something and the Bible says, "God made you to love you." You were created as an object of God's love. If you want to know why you're taking breath right now, why your heart is beating, it's because you were made to be loved by God and to bring Him glory.

Now, God wants you to learn to love Him back and that's the first purpose of your life. One day, Jesus was walking down the street and a man came up and said, "What's the most important command in the Bible?" And Jesus said, "I'm going to summarize the entire Bible in one sentence. Love God with all your heart and soul and mind and strength." That's called the great commandment. And God wants you to get to know and love Him back. That means, when you get up in the morning, you should sit on the side of your bed and say, "God, if I don't get anything else done today, I want to know you a little bit better and I want to love you a little bit more." Because, if at the end of the day you know God more and you love Him more, you have just fulfilled one of the purposes of your life.

If, on the other hand, you've accomplished all kinds of things and achieved many, many successes in life, but at the end of the day you don't know God better or love Him more, you have missed the primary purpose of your life. God didn't put you on this earth just to mark things off of your to-do list. He put you here to know Him and love Him. That's why you exist.

Does my life really matter?

Well, that's a good question. Today, we teach our children that we're all just one big cosmic accident. We came from the goo through the zoo to you over billions of years. Well, if that is true, in a nutshell, it teaches that your life really doesn't matter, you're just the freak accident of random chance, you're complex slime and you were an accident. And, if you were accidentally killed, well, of course, that doesn't matter. This creates a lot of our sociological problems and a lot of our self-esteem issues.

But the truth is, you are not an accident. You were created by a loving God who loves you and designed you with intricate detail in your life. When you understand that, God made you to love yourself and others and that God made you to be a part of His family and that God made you to last forever, then you're never going to have a problem with low self-esteem again.

Truthfully, if there is no God, then your life doesn't matter. However because there is a God, God had a specific purpose in mind when He created you and you do matter. You matter because he sent His Son, Jesus Christ, to die on the cross for you. If you want to know how much you matter, think of Jesus Christ with his arms outstretched saying, "I love you this much."

Now, if you had to choose between a loved one and a material thing, even if that thing was priceless, you'd choose your loved one in a heartbeat. And when you're on your deathbed, you're not going to surround yourself with material possessions, you're not going to say, "Bring me my trophies. Bring me my credentials. Bring me my certificates so I can look one more time at my grade point average." No. You're going to surround yourself with loved ones and everybody's going to be crying because they're going to miss you. You see, that's how much you matter.

Personal relationships with God and other people are the most important thing in life. God wants you to know Him and He wants you to have a relationship with Him because you're worth so much in God's eyes that he sent His Son to die for you. I hope you'll get to know Him very soon.

Is there a real hell and why would a loving God send anyone there?

First, I believe in hell because Jesus talked about it. In fact, Jesus talked more about hell than He did heaven. He said it is a real place and it is a place of eternal torment. And I believe Jesus knows more about it than either you or I.

Secondly, I believe in hell because logic and fairness demand it. Think of all the atrocities and evil that have been done throughout history by evildoers in this world. For God to allow those crimes to go unpunished would mean that God is not worthy of our worship and love.

Now why would a loving God send anyone to hell? Well in a nutshell, God doesn't. God doesn't send anybody to hell. We choose to go there when we reject the love of God. If I were to say to my right is a door heading to heaven, and to my left is a door heading to hell, if you walk out the door heading to hell, you don't have anybody to blame but yourself.

In fact, the Bible tells us that God does almost everything — well everything possible to keep us out of hell. He cared so much to keep us out of hell that he sent Jesus Christ to come to earth, to die on the cross, to pay

Unveiling Your Inner Light

for our sins so that we don't have to pay for them. He wants to set us free. He wants to give us forgiveness. God made us in his image and He gave us the ultimate power to say yes or no.

If we choose to reject God here on earth, then we, at the same time, are choosing to spend eternity separated from Him. There are only two kinds people in the world. Those who say, "Thy will be done here to God on earth" and those to whom God says, "Your will be done," when we say, "I want to do it my way." And if we say, "God I don't want you in my life while I'm here on earth," then God says, "I don't want you in my heaven for eternity."

You don't have to go to hell. In fact, Jesus Christ has made it possible for you to go to heaven. Open your heart to Him and say, "Jesus Christ, I need you, I want you, I trust you and I ask you to forgive me." And He'll come in and save you.

Chapter 8
How You Can Survive a Satanic Attack!

When we hear the word 'war', we think of physical combat with armored vehicles, soldiers in uniform, and deadly weapons. Yet, there is a spiritual war going on around us that is just as dangerous; one we often ignore or fail to understand. We have a powerful opponent working against us. In fact, the Lord calls him "the god of this age" (2 Cor. 4:4) because he is the source of evil and wickedness in our world. To overcome Satan's attacks, we must first recognize that he is a real adversary. Then we need to hold our ground against him. To stand firm, we have to dress for battle.

First, You Identify the Enemy (Satan).

Second, Stand Firm against the attack:

- Don't give in
- Don't give up
- Don't say "I am weak"
- Don't debate
- Don't argue

Satan doesn't look like a terrible monster or dark cloud and tempt you or make you angry. In fact, he does what he can to disguise himself and make himself invisible so he won't be blamed or fought as the enemy. He will manipulate circumstances and situations against you. He will use people against you-people who will abuse you, misuse you, and confuse you! Satan's purpose is to steal, kill and to destroy.

Satan can set up a series of good things to lead you down the path he desires for you to walk, a path that is away from God and toward self.

The devil doesn't really care how much good you experience as long as you become so wrapped up in that good feeling or good time that you fail to see that your life is about to go over a cliff.

He has a goal: to destroy your Body, Mind, or spirit, or all three. He seeks to get us off track and out of the will of God for our lives. The Devil is a master at causing misunderstandings.

You must pray and ask God to give you discernment. Prayer gives us greater discernment. It is in prayer, and as the result of prayer, that we are able to see what others don't see. We especially are able to see the lies of the devil for what they are. Prayer is also our foremost way of hearing God speak in our hearts, to give us warning or forewarning of something. It may be something little or big. We need to pay attention to the still, small voice of God warning us.

Ask God for help in discerning between good and evil, between what is real and what is illusion, between what is good and what is best and most importantly between our desires and God's plan.

We open ourselves up to attacks (financial, marriage problems, problems on job, accidents) when we don't recognize evil for what it is, when we don't see the true reality of a situation, when we settle for less than God's best, and when we mistake our desires for God's desires.

Many people have failed to receive God's best in their lives because they settled for what seemed to be "good".

God doesn't want you to have a mediocre job that you hate getting up and going to everyday. He doesn't want you to have an average marriage. He doesn't want you to have just a little bit of peace in your life. NO! God desires for you to feel fulfilled and overjoyed in your life. He wants you to experience HIS highest and Best!

Satan's Fiery Darts

The apostle Paul wrote that we who are in Christ are going to face all the fiery darts of the wicked one (Eph.6:16). God's desire is that we be able to distinguish all the flaming arrows that the devil sends our way. What are these flaming arrows?

- Fear
- Doubt
- Lust
- Loneliness
- Jealousy
- Rejection
- Guilt
- Greed or Covetousness
- Unforgiveness
- Anger
- Discouragement
- Pride

Many people ask, "Does the devil have excess to my mind?" YES

Can the devil send thoughts into my mind? YES

Can the devil speak to the heart? YES

The Devil does not send the same thoughts to every person. The devil knows your area of weakness and needs. He crafts his messages specifically for you.

If Satan is capable of deceiving you, craftily manipulating you, and seducing you to yield to temptation in one area of your life, he's going to come back again and again to that area. He has identified this as an area of weakness in your life. The more times he successfully tempts you in this area, the weaker that area becomes. This area of weakness in you becomes a spiritual stronghold for him! What is weakness in you is a strong place for him to work in your life.

Third, Put on the Full armor of God, so you can stand firm:

One of the most important passages in the Bible about overcoming enemy attacks is found in Eph.6:10-18.

Pray this prayer every morning and every chance you get. Now, Satan will say to you "You don't need to pray about this" and "You don't have time to Pray" etc… The devil is a liar about Prayer!

Putting on your Armor

Lord, by faith here's what I'm doing right now to prepare myself for the coming day. I'm on the belt of truth. I ask you to make it very clear to me what I am to accept into my life and what I am to reject. Help me to see clearly the motives of others as they deal with me and converse with me. Let me walk in YOUR truth, making decisions and choices according to your plans and purposes for my life.

I am putting on the breastplate of righteousness. Guard my emotions today. Protect my heart. Help me to take into my life only the things that are pure, and nothing that is poison or polluting. Help me to live in integrity and to have a reputation based upon doings, sayings, believing, thinking, and feeling the right things. Help me to live in the right relationship with you every moment of this coming day.

I am putting on my spiritual boots. Help me to stand and walk in Your peace and to move forward in ways that bring Your peace and love to others. Help me to have full confidence and assurance that come from knowing that I am filled with the peace that only you can give to those who are your children. Help me to be a peacemaker. Show me where to walk and how to walk as you would walk.

I am picking up the shield of faith. Help me to trust you to be my Victor in every area of my life today. Help me to trust you to defend me,

Unveiling Your Inner Light

provide for me, and keep me in safety every hour of this day.

I am putting on my helmet of salvation. Guard my mind today. Bring to my remembrance all that you have done for me as my Savoir. Let me live in the hope and confidence that you are saving me, rescuing me and delivering me from evil.

I am picking up my sword of the spirit, the word of God. Bring to my remembrance today the verses of the Bible that I have read and memorized, and help me to apply them to the situations and circumstances I will face. Let me use your word to bring your light into the darkness of this world and to defeat the devil when he comes to tempt me.

Father, I want to be fully clothed with the identity of Jesus Christ today. I am in Christ. He is in me. Help me to fully realize and accept that he is my truth, my righteousness, my peace, my Savior, the source of my faith, and the ever-present Lord of my life.

I want to bring glory to your name today. I ask all of this in the name of Jesus, Amen.

Chapter 9
Prayer Changes things

For all Christians, praying is very important, because it makes their relationship with God stronger, and they believe it changes them and the world in which they live.

Prayer is often seen by Christians as "talking to God." It is one of the main activities in the life of a Christian. There are no set rules one must follow. We must come to God as we are. Still, the New Testament gives many instructions about prayer. The greatest key to spiritual growth is spending time alone with the Lord. This means taking the time to speak with God about whatever is on your heart and, even more importantly, allowing Him to speak to you.

Jesus makes clear that prayer is always about the intention. The heart is important; it should be focused on God. It's not about the words or the gestures people make. That perhaps might impress people, but God sees whether we are sincere or not. Above all, pray with sincerity, honor, and humbleness before the Almighty God. "The earnest prayer of a righteous person has great power and wonderful results" (James 5:16).

It has been well said that God always answers prayer. Sometimes He says, "Yes." sometimes He says, "NO." Sometimes he says wait because the timing is not right. If he says no it is because he has something better in store for you or it is for your protection. Whatever the reason, he knows all. The Bible teaches, among other things, that if we pray with doubt, we will not get an answer (James 1:6-7). We need to pray with faith and a pure heart believing God will answer. One of the things you should pray is that God will confirm your spiritual gift. Once you have taken the spiritual gifts test make sure you ask God to confirm that the gifts you feel are your own will be validated and he will. You will know in your inner spirit that you have those particular gifts. Below you will find many different samples of prayers I use myself.

Prayer of Salvation:

Father, it is written in your word that if I confess with my mouth that Jesus is Lord and believe in my heart that you have raised him from the dead, I shall be saved. Therefore, Father, I confess that Jesus is my Lord. I make him Lord of my life right now. I believe in my heart that you raised Jesus from the dead. I renounce my past life with Satan and close the door to any of his devices. I thank you for forgiving me of all my sin. Jesus is my Lord, and I am a new creation. Old things have passed away. Now all things become new in Jesus' name, Amen

Romans 10: 9-10
John 3:17
2 Corinthians 5:17
John 17:3

Prosperity Affirmation

I am blessed, and I am a blessing. Everything I lay my hand to prospers and succeeds. I am blessed when I come in and blessed when I go out. I have favor everywhere I go. God is multiplying me. I seek first the kingdom of God and he adds all other things I need. I love to give. I always have plenty of seed to sow and bread to eat. My cup runs over. Goodness and mercy follow me all the days of my life. I always have more than enough.

Genesis 17:2
Deuteronomy 28:6, 8, 11-13 & 29:9 & 30:9
Ecclesiastes 11:1
Psalm 118:25
Proverbs 10:22 & 3:9-10 & 11:25 & 28:25
Philippians 4:19

Protection Prayer:

Father God, in the name of Jesus I come to you asking for a hedge of protection. I thank you, Father that you are a wall of fire round about me and that you set your angels round about me as well.

I thank you, Father that I dwell in the secret place of the most high and abide under the shadow of the almighty. I say of you, Lord, You are my refuge and my fortress, in you I will trust. You cover me with your feathers, and under your wings shall I trust. I will not be afraid of the terror by night or the fiery dart that flies by day. Your truth will be my shield and protection. I will not be afraid of diseases that come in the dark or sickness that strikes at noon. At my side one thousand people may die, or even ten thousand right beside me, but I will not be hurt.

Because you have made me Lord, you are my refuge and fortress, NO evil shall befall me- No accident will overtake me-neither shall any plague or calamity come near my home. For you give your ANGELS charge over me, to keep me in all your ways. They are encamped around about me. The Lord is my light and the one who saves me. I will fear no one. The Lord protects my life.

Father, because you have set your love upon me, therefore will you deliver me. I will call upon you, and you will answer me. You will be with me in trouble, and will satisfy me with long life and show me your salvation. NOT one hair on my head shall perish. Thank you Jesus, Amen.

Jeremiah 1:12
Psalm 91:1-2, 10-11
Psalm 127:2
Isaiah 49:25
Mark 4:35
Proverbs 3: 5, 23-24

Prayer for Finances

Heavenly Father, most Gracious and Loving God, I pray to you that you abundantly bless My family and me. I know that you recognize, that a Family Is more than just a mother, father, sister, brother, cousin, Husband

Spiritual Gifts _____

Unveiling Your Inner Light

and wife, but all who believe and trust in You.

Dear GOD, I send up a prayer request for Financial blessing for not only the Person who

Is reading this prayer but whomever they are standing in the gap for. And that the power of joined prayer by Those who Believe and trust in you is More powerful than anything!

I thank you in Advance for your blessings. God, deliver the person reading this right Now

from debt and debt burdens. Release your Godly wisdom that I may be a Good steward over all that you have given me GOD, for I know how wonderful and mighty You are and how if we just obey you and walk In your word and have the faith of a Mustard Seed that you will pour out blessings.

I thank you now Lord for the recent blessings I have Received and for the blessings yet to come, Because I know you are not done with me yet. In Jesus name Amen...

Prayer for Employment

Heavenly Father, more than ever before, people are in need of the sustaining power of Your grace. For you once promised us that just as You looked over the birds and flowers of the fields, so would You provide for us, and more, if we would but beseech your divine generosity.

Lord, we come before you now because you are our only rock in a shifting and dangerous sea. We place our faith in you alone, because we know from whence all gifts ultimately come. Look down on the father who is wondering how to keep a roof over his family's head. Lift up the mother who is wondering how she will keep food on the table. Have mercy on the children who, through no fault of their own, go without.

We pray these things in the name of Jesus. Amen.

Spiritual Gifts

Unveiling Your Inner Light

Victory over Depression:

Father, you are my refuge and my high tower and my stronghold in times of trouble. I lean on and confidently put my trust in you, for you have not forsaken me. I seek you on the authority of your word and the right of my necessity. I praise you, the help of my countenance and my God.

Lord, you lift up those who are bowed down. Therefore, I am strong and my heart takes courage. I establish myself on righteousness- right standing in conformity with your will and order. I am far even from the thought of oppression or destruction, for I fear not. I am far from terror for it shall not come near me.

Father, you have thoughts and plans for my welfare and peace. My mind is stayed on you, for I stop allowing myself to be agitated and disturbed and intimidated and cowardly and unsettled.

"In the name of Jesus I loose my mind from wrong thought patterns. I tear down strongholds that have protected bad perceptions about myself. I submit to you, Father, and resist fear, discouragement, self-pity and depression. I will not give place to the devil by harboring depression, and will continue to be an overcomer by the word of my testimony and the blood of the Lamb." resentment and holding onto anger. I surround myself with songs and shouts of deliverance from

Father, I thank you that I have been given a spirit of power and of Love and of a calm and well-balanced mind. I have discipline and self-control. I have the mind of Christ and hold the thoughts, feelings, and purposed of His heart. I have a fresh mental and spiritual attitude, for I am constantly renewed in the spirit of my mind with your word, Father.

Therefore, I brace up and reinvigorate and cut through and make firm and straight paths for my feet- safe and upright and happy paths that go in the right direction. I arise from depression and prostration in which circumstances have kept me. I rise to new life: I shine and am radiant with the glory of the Lord.

Thank You, Father, in Jesus' name, that I am set free from every evil work. I praise you that the joy of the Lord is my strength and stronghold! Hallelujah!

Prayer over Sickness

Lord I come before you asking for health and healing in the name of Jesus right now for _____. I believe that healing is in his/her veins and by Jesus stripes he/she has been healed of all infirmities and sickness. I decree and declare supernatural healing of all sickness, disease and ill things from hell. It is bound, null and void in the mighty name of Jesus, I walk by faith and not by sight, I don't care what the lab results say or what the doctor says, I care about God's last word! I Thank you Jesus for your mighty hand. Thank you for your deliverance and the miracle of resurrection. I loosen healing, restoration, wholeness and holiness over ___ right now in Jesus name. Thank you for your infinite peace and divine intervention.

Healing Prayer

Father in the name of Jesus, I confess your word concerning healing. As I do this, I believe and say that your word will not return to you void, but will accomplish what it says it will. Therefore, I believe in the name of Jesus that I am healed, according to 1 peter 2:24. It is written in your word that Jesus himself took our infirmities and bore our sicknesses.

Therefore, with great boldness and confidence I say on the authority of that written word that I am redeemed from the curse of sickness, and I refuse to tolerate it's symptoms. No evil shall befall me, no plague or calamity shall come near my dwelling.

I confess the word of God abides in me and delivers to me perfect soundness of mind and wholeness in body and spirit from the deepest parts of my nature in my immortal spirit even to the joints and marrow of my bones. I stand immovable and fixed in full assurance that I have health and healing now in the name of Jesus.

Spiritual Gifts

Unveiling Your Inner Light

Jesus Promises Healing

Jesus told His disciples that He will do as they ask. He reminds them that their Father in Heaven cares for them just as our earthly father cares for us. Matthew 7:7-11 "Ask, and it will be given to you; seek, and you will find; knock, and it will be opened to you. For everyone who asks receives, and the one who seeks finds, and to the one who knocks it will be opened. Or which one of you, if his son asks him for bread, will give him a stone? Or if he asks for a fish, will give him a serpent? If you then, who are evil, know how to give good gifts to your children, how much more will your Father who is in heaven give good things to those who ask him!"

Jesus warns that unforgiveness in a man's heart will hinder the prayer for healing.

Mark 11:23-26 "Truly, I say to you, whoever says to this mountain, 'Be taken up and thrown into the sea,' and does not doubt in his heart, but believes that what he says will come to pass, it will be done for him. Therefore I tell you, whatever you ask in prayer, believe that you have received it, and it will be yours. And whenever you stand praying, forgive, if you have anything against anyone, so that your Father also who is in heaven may forgive you your trespasses."

Jesus reminds his disciples that the gift of healing was given to the Apostles as a sign to the unbeliever. Our prayers for healing will show unbelievers that our God is the Healer even today.

Mark 16:18 "And these signs will accompany those who believe: in my name they will cast out demons; they will speak in new tongues; they will pick up serpents with their hands; and if they drink any deadly poison, it will not hurt them; they will lay their hands on the sick, and they will recover."

Jesus promises that when we maintain our relationship with Him and we remember that He is the One who heals, He will do it. John 15:7 "If you abide in me, and my words abide in you, ask whatever you wish, and it will be done for you."

Examples of People Who Were Healed:

Matthew 9:20-22 And behold, a woman who had suffered from a discharge of blood for twelve years came up behind him and touched the fringe of his garment, for she said to herself, "If I only touch his garment, I will be made well." Jesus turned, and seeing her he said, "Take heart, daughter; your faith has made you well." And instantly the woman was made well.

Mark 2:8-12 And immediately Jesus, perceiving in his spirit that they thus questioned within themselves, said to them, "Why do you question these things in your hearts? Which is easier, to say to the paralytic, 'Your sins are forgiven,' or to say, 'Rise, take up your bed and walk'? But that you may know that the Son of Man has authority on earth to forgive sins"—he said to the paralytic— "I say to you, rise, pick up your bed, and go home." And he rose and immediately picked up his bed and went out before them all, so that they were all amazed and glorified God, saying, "We never saw anything like this!"

Luke 17:11-19 On the way to Jerusalem he was passing along between Samaria and Galilee. And as he entered a village, he was met by ten lepers, who stood at a distance and lifted up their voices, saying, "Jesus, Master, have mercy on us." When he saw them he said to them, "Go and show yourselves to the priests." And as they went they were cleansed. Then one of them, when he saw that he was healed, turned back, praising God with a loud voice; and he fell on his face at Jesus' feet, giving him thanks. Now he was a Samaritan. Then Jesus answered, "Were not ten cleansed? Where are the nine? Was no one found to return and give praise to God except this foreigner?" And he said to him, "Rise and go your way; your faith has made you well."

John 9:1-7 As he passed by, he saw a man blind from birth. And his disciples asked him, "Rabbi, who sinned, this man or his parents, that he was born blind?" Jesus answered, "It was not that this man sinned, or his parents, but that the works of God might be displayed in him. We must work the works of him who sent me while it is day; night is coming, when no one can work. As long as I am in the world, I am the light of the world."

Spiritual Gifts

Unveiling Your Inner Light

Having said these things, he spit on the ground and made mud with the saliva. Then he anointed the man's eyes with the mud and said to him, "Go, wash in the pool of Siloam" (which means Sent). So he went and washed and came back seeing.

Acts 9:40-42 But Peter put them all outside, and knelt down and prayed; and turning to the body he said, "Tabitha, arise." And she opened her eyes, and when she saw Peter she sat up. And he gave her his hand and raised her up. Then calling the saints and widows, he presented her alive. And it became known throughout all Joppa, and many believed in the Lord.

Acts 14:8-10 Now at Lystra there was a man sitting who could not use his feet. He was crippled from birth and had never walked. He listened to Paul speaking. And Paul, looking intently at him and seeing that he had faith to be made well, said in a loud voice, "Stand upright on your feet." And he sprang up and began walking.

Prayers for Worry and Stress

1. Heaven Father, I cast the whole of my care—all anxieties, worries and concerns—upon you once and for all. I know you love me and care for me. I make all my requests known to you with thanksgiving. Because I know you hear me, I believe your "best" answers are on the way the moment I pray, in the name of Jesus Amen.

2. Father, You have created me to live this life as a leader—above and not beneath. With your help, I will be the head and not the tail. Always at the top! NEVER at the bottom! Filled with counsel and might, not with doubt, despair and defeat. In the name of Jesus, I will complete every assignment you give me, Lord, because I am infused with your ability! Hallelujah!

3. Father, in Jesus' name there is NO bondage this side of heaven that can get a grip on me! You have set me free with your outstretched arm. Thank you for redeeming me. Thank you for liberating me from the works of the devil. Thank you for walking with me each day. Thank you for

keeping me free through the power of the Holy Spirit. Amen

A Prayer for My Husband/ Wife (Desire for Marriage)

Father I believe that you are providing your very best for me and the man who will be united with me in marriage. This mighty man of valor has awakened to righteousness. Father as you have rejoiced over Jerusalem, so shall the bridegroom rejoice over me. Thank you Father that he will love me as Christ loves the Church. He will nourish, carefully protect and cherish me. I ask that you bless him now wherever he is with your divine favor, an unlimited anointing to fulfill his purpose and destiny in you. I ask that you increase his strength, revive and refresh his spirit. I ask that you that you give him deeper and greater understanding of you Father and your Word I ask that you grant him clarity in his spiritual sight and hearing. I ask that you give him seed to sow into your kingdom and that his harvest be bountiful.

Father I believe, because he is your best, that doubt wavering and insincerity are not a part of him; but he speaks your oracles, God, acknowledging your full council with all wisdom and knowledge. He does not speak or act contrary to the Word. He walks totally in love esteeming and preferring others higher than himself.

Father I believe that everything that is not of you shall be removed from my life. And, I thank you for the perfecting of your Word in my life that I may be thoroughly furnished unto all good works. Father I praise you for the performance of your word on my behalf. Father I believe that you are grooming me to be a suitable helpmate for my husband. According to your Word I will adapt myself to my husband, respect, honor, prefer and esteem him, stand firmly by his side, united in spirit and purpose, having the same love and being in full accord and of one harmonious mind and intention. Lord teach me to be a wise, understanding and prudent wife that my husband will find favor of you. I know that my future husband has found favor in your sight, and I praise you and thank you for your Word, knowing that you watch over it to perform it.

Spiritual Gifts _____

Unveiling Your Inner Light

Father I declare by faith that we shun immorality and all sexual looseness. We flee from impurity in thought, word and deed. We will honor you God and bring glory to you in our spirit, soul and bodies, which are yours, God. Lord I pray that you allow our meeting/courtship and marriage to glorify you in every way. May our family be seen as bright lights, stars or beacons shining out clear in a dark world.

Father in the name of Jesus, it is written in your Word that love is shed abroad in our hearts by the Holy Spirit who is given to us. Because you are in us, we acknowledge that Love reigns supreme. We believe that love is displayed in full expression enfolding and knitting us together in truth, making us perfect for the good work to do your will, working in us that which is good and pleasing in your sight.

Father because you are concerned with everything that concerns us, I ask that you conform me, my body and personal style to the liking of my husband and likewise he unto me that we will continually desire to drink from our own cistern and be utterly satisfied physically, emotionally and mentally. Father let the same attitude and humble mind be in me and my intended mate which is in Christ Jesus.

I believe and pray that we will conduct our marriage and ourselves honorably and becomingly. We esteem it as precious, worthy and of great price. We commit ourselves to live in mutual harmony and accord with one another delighting in each other, being of the same mind and united in spirit.

Father we believe and say that we are gentle, compassionate, courteous, tenderhearted and humble minded. We seek peace, and it keeps our hearts in quietness and assurance. Because we follow after love and dwell in peace, our prayers are not hindered in any way. We are heirs together of the grace of God.

I declare by faith that our marriage grows stronger day by day in the bond of unity because it is founded on your Word and rooted and grounded in your love.

Father I confess and pray that I will stand by my husband's side and under gird him in prayer, I will say only that thing that will edify him. I will not allow myself to judge him but I continue to intercede for him and speak and pray blessings upon him in the name of Jesus. I thank you for the performance of your Word, in Jesus' name. Amen.

CHAPTER 10
Situational Prayers and Scriptures

Stress

God understands exactly how frazzled we can feel as we rush about in our very busy lives. Sometimes, it seems as though everything is against us, yet God is willing to help. But first, we must seek God and choose to allow Him into our lives; to be our guide and our comfort.

In today's world, it is virtually impossible to avoid some sort of stress. Almost everyone is carrying some amount of it, in varying degrees. Many find it more and more difficult to simply survive in the world we live in. There are so many desperate people that many are seeking relief for their problems through any remedy they can find. Our culture is inundated with self-help books, therapists, time-management workshops, massage parlors, and recovery programs (to name just the tip of the iceberg). Everyone talks about returning to a "simpler" way of life, but no one seems to even know exactly what that means, or how to attain it.

Most of us are so used to carrying the burden of stress, that mainly we think it is simply an unavoidable part of living in the world. We carry it like an experienced hiker with a huge pack on his back. The pack seems to be a part of his own weight, and he can't even remember what it was ever like to not be carrying it. It seems that his legs have always been that heavy and his back has always ached under all the weight. Only when he stops to rest for a moment and takes off his pack does he realize just how heavy it really is, and how light and free he is without it.

Unfortunately, most of us cannot just unload stress like a backpack. It seems to be inherently woven into the very fabric of our lives. It harbors somewhere beneath our skin (usually in a knot between our shoulder blades). It keeps us up late into the night, just when we need sleep the most. It presses in on us from all sides. Yet, Jesus says, "Come to me all you who are weary and burdened, and I will give you rest. Take my yoke upon you and learn from me, for I am gentle and humble in heart and you will find rest for your souls. For my yoke is easy and my burden is light." (Mt. 11:28-30). Those words have touched the hearts of many, yet they are only words that merely sound comforting and are, in essence, worthless, unless they are true. If they are true, how can we apply them to our lives and walk free from the burdens that weigh us down so badly? Perhaps you are responding, "I would love do that if only I knew how!" How can we receive rest for our souls?

Much of the stress that we carry springs from the fact that we don't know who we are or where we are going or even our purpose, for that matter. Even Christians who know that ultimately they are going to heaven when they die, are still anxious in this lifetime because they do not really know who they are in Christ and who Christ is in them. No matter who we are, we are bound to have tribulation in this life. It is unavoidable, but having trouble in this life is not the issue anyway. The real issue is how we react to it. That is where stress ultimately comes from. The trials we face in this world will either break us or make us strong.

The first thing we must do to be free from our stress and our worry is to come unto Jesus. Without Him, our life has no real purpose or depth. We simply run from one activity to another, seeking to fill our lives with some sort of meaning, purpose, peace, and happiness. "Who we are under pressure reveals who we really are. The storms of life wash away the thin veneer that we present to the world and expose what lies in our heart. God, in His mercy, allows the storms to hit us so we will turn to Him and be cleansed of the sin that we were never able to perceive in times of ease. We can either turn to Him and receive a soft heart in the midst of all our trials, or we can turn away and harden our heart. The hard times in life will either make us pliable and merciful, full of faith in God, or angry and brittle, full of doubt and unbelief.

As you already know, there will be times when we all face incredibly difficult circumstances that have an awesome power to destroy us. The best way to counteract stress in those times, is to begin to praise God and thank Him for His countless blessings in our lives. The old saying "count your blessings" really is true. In spite of everything, there are so many blessings woven throughout our lives that many of us do not even have the eyes to see them. Even if your situation seems hopeless, God is still worthy of all your praise. God delights in a heart that will praise Him no matter what your bank statement says, our family says, our time schedule says, or any other circumstance that would try to exalt itself against the knowledge of God. As we praise and bless the name of the Most High, everything else in this world begins to pale and fade away against the sheer loveliness of who He is.

Scriptures to help you deal with stress:

"Casting all your anxiety on Him, because He cares for you."

1 Peter 5:7

"No temptation has overtaken you but such as is common to man; and God is faithful, who will not allow you to be tempted beyond what you are able, but with the temptation will provide the way of escape also, so that you will be able to endure it."

1 Corinthians 10:13

"Anxiety in a man's heart weighs it down, but a good word makes it glad."

Proverbs 12:25

"Let your light shine before men in such a way that they may see your good works, and glorify your Father who is in heaven."

Matthew 5:16

"I will lift up my eyes to the mountains; from whence shall my help come? My help comes from the LORD, who made heaven and earth. He will not allow your foot to slip; He who keeps you will not slumber. Behold, He who keeps Israel will neither slumber nor sleep.

"The LORD is your keeper; the LORD is your shade on your right hand.

Spiritual Gifts
Unveiling Your Inner Light

The sun will not smite you by day, nor the moon by night. The LORD will protect you from all evil; He will keep your soul. The LORD will guard your going out and your coming in from this time forth and forever."

Psalm 121:1-8

"In everything give thanks; for this is God's will for you in Christ Jesus."

1 Thessalonians 5:18

"Be anxious for nothing, but in everything by prayer and supplication with thanksgiving let your requests be made known to God. And the peace of God, which surpasses all comprehension, will guard your hearts and your minds in Christ Jesus."

Philippians 4:6-7

"Peace I leave with you; My peace I give to you; not as the world gives do I give to you. Do not let your heart be troubled, nor let it be fearful."

John 14:27

"God is our refuge and strength, a very present help in trouble. Therefore we will not fear, though the earth should change and though the mountains slip into the heart of the sea; though its waters roar and foam, though the mountains quake at its swelling pride."

Psalm 46:1-3

"The LORD also will be a stronghold for the oppressed, a stronghold in times of trouble; and those who know Your name will put their trust in You, for You, O LORD, have not forsaken those who seek You." Psalm 9:9-10

God's Guidance

The declaration of Scripture is that God cares about each of us and wants to direct our lives. How infinitely superior His plan must be in every detail with all the wisdom and data He possesses, past, present, and future, and with all the power at His disposal as the sovereign God of the universe. The greatest evidence of God's desire to guide our lives is found in the fact of the Scriptures. He has given us the Bible so that we might know His will and purpose in all areas of life. This means knowing God and the life He has for us to live. Our responsibility, by God's own direction, is to entrust our way to Him for His direction and leading.

As you think about God's will, what comes to mind? It has been my experience that many people generally focus on certain things, but ignore the more basic and important areas. For example, guidance or finding God's will is often restricted to such things as:

- Who do I marry?
- Where do I work?
- What car should I buy?
- What house should I buy?
- Should I go to college, and if so, where should I go?

As is obvious, when such a list is the primary focus, guidance becomes something people want for their own happiness and fulfillment so life will flow along smoothly like. Certainly we should seek God's guidance and pray about such things as James warned us when he wrote, "Instead, you ought to say, 'If the Lord wills, we shall live and also do this or that'" (James 4:15). In a similar fashion, Paul wrote, "and I always ask in my prayers, if perhaps now at last I may succeed in visiting you according to the will of God." (Rom. 1:10), and Proverbs 16:3 says, "Commit your works to the LORD, and your plans will be established."

The Bible is full of instructions as to how God wants his people to live. It speaks of our relationship with God himself, the place of prayer and his word in our lives, and how to grow in that relationship. It talks about relationships in the home, relationships with other believers, how we should treat our enemies, our attitude to our boss and employees, what we should do with the gifts God has given us, the virtues we should seek to develop in our characters, etc. We don't need any special guidance to find out God's will about these things. All we need do is to read the Bible regularly and prayerfully and seek to obey the things that God teaches us from it. Much of God's will has already been made plain. It may not be easy to obey, but that is another issue. Mark Twain once said, "It is not the things in the Bible that I don't understand that trouble me, but the things I do understand!" God gives us the Holy Spirit for the very purpose of enabling us to obey.

A look at those passages where God's will is specifically mentioned, shows that our own happiness and the details with which we are so often occupied are secondary, never primary. Such an occupation or attitude typifies the shallow thinking of a society that is out of touch with the purposes of the living God and how He works. We are a consumer-oriented society bent on our own comfort and pleasure, whereas God has much greater goals in mind.

Just a brief glance at passages where the words "will of God" are found quickly show us God's primary concern is in the realm of the spiritual and concerns the moral will of God or Christ-like change.

Scriptures for Guidance:

Psalm 37: 4-5

Delight yourself in the Lord and he will give you the desires of your heart. Commit your way to the Lord; trust in him and he will do this.

Psalm 77:13-14

Your ways, O God, are holy. What God is so great as our God? You are the God who performs miracles; you display your power among the peoples.

Psalm 31: 3

Since you are my rock and my fortress, for the sake of your name lead and guide me.

Psalm 48: 14

For this God is for ever and ever; he will be our guide even to the end.

Psalm 73: 23-24

Yet, I am always with you; you hold me by my right hand. You guide me with your counsel, and afterward you will take me into glory.

Psalm 139: 9-10

If I rise on the wings of the dawn, if I settle on the far side of the sea, even there your hand will guide me, your right hand will hold me fast.

Romans 8: 25-28

But if we hope for what we do not yet have, we wait for it patiently. In the same way, the spirit helps us in our weakness. We do not know what we ought to pray for, but the spirit himself intercedes for us with groans that words cannot express. And he who searches our hearts knows the mind of the spirit, because the spirit intercedes for the saints in accordance with God's will. And we know that in all things God works for the good of those who love him, who have been called according to his purpose.

Philippians 4: 6-7

Do not be anxious about anything, but in everything, by prayer and petition, with thanksgiving, present your requests to God. And the peace of God, which transcends all understanding, will guard your hearts and your minds in Christ Jesus.

Psalm 32: 8

I will instruct you and teach you in the way you should go; I will counsel you and watch over you. Do not be like the horse or mule, which have no understanding but must be controlled by bit and bridle or they will not come to you.

Psalm 37: 23, 24, 31

If the Lord delights in a man's way, he makes his steps firm; though he stumble, he will not fall, for the Lord upholds him with his hand. The Law of his God is in his heart; his feet do not slip.

Isaiah 41: 10, 13

So do not fear, for I am with you; do not be dismayed, for I am your God. I will strengthen you and help you; I will uphold you with my righteous right hand. For I am the Lord your God, who takes hold of your right hand and says to you, do not fear; I will help you.

Isaiah 42: 16

I will lead the blind by ways they have not known, along unfamiliar paths I will guide them; I will turn the darkness into light before them and make the rough places smooth. These things I will do; I will not forsake them.

Despair

God is our help, refuge and deliverer. Please know God is always with us, even when things seem like they are beyond crazy. Call upon God. Rest, trust and believe in God. Put your eyes and your focus on God, fill your heart and mind with the word of God. God is our deliverance. He loves us more than anybody can or will. We should always ask God to direct our footsteps, and we should seek God's direction. May you feel the peace and presence of God in your life. May you hear God's voice and be comforted and strengthened, with renewed hope. It is also very important to surround yourself with godly people (friends, relatives, etc.) that will encourage you and help you focus on God. May God provide people that will stand by you and encourage you as you pass through the fire.

Spiritual Gifts

Unveiling Your Inner Light

Scripture recognizes and validates the reality and the depth of suffering and evil. Scripture allows us to grieve and mourn when necessary and appropriate. But, Scripture does not let us stay there; we are not to despair of all hope. Suffering is real, but is it never the last word.

For Christians in a fallen world, it's sometimes too easy to have anxiety or fall into a depression. We've all been there at one time or another, but it doesn't have to be that way. Family, friends, jobs, and other factors can bring us down… but just remember, that nothing should ever make you feel like you should hurt yourself. Remember that you are one of God's children, and He loves you dearly.

God will always heal your broken heart and heal your wounds - turn to Him if you are having troubles in your life. The cure might not be instantaneous, but He will help you find the path to happiness. Christ strengthens all of us - so put your faith in Him!

The Bible is the book you need to overcome depression and live the joyous, prosperous life that you deserve and that the Lord wants you to live. So please read these Bible verses on depression if you're having a hard time dealing with life. You're not the only one and you have a God that LOVES you - you will feel better once you realize it!

Scripture references to help you with Despair:

"We are afflicted in every way, but not crushed; perplexed, but not despairing; persecuted, but not forsaken; struck down, but not destroyed."
2 Corinthians 4:8-9

"Therefore we do not lose heart, but though our outer man is decaying, yet our inner man is being renewed day by day. For momentary, light affliction is producing for us an eternal weight of glory far beyond all comparison, while we look not at the things which are seen, but at the things which are not seen; for the things which are seen are temporal, but the things which are not seen are eternal."
2 Corinthians 4:17-18

"Make sure that your character is free from the love of money, being content with what you have; for He Himself has said, 'I will never desert you, nor will I ever forsake you,' so that we confidently say, 'The Lord is my helper, I will not be afraid. What will man do to me.'"
Hebrews 13:5-6

"Come to Me, all who are weary and heavy-laden, and I will give you rest. Take My yoke upon you and learn from Me, for I am gentle and humble in heart, and you will find rest for your souls. For My yoke is easy and My burden is light."
Matthew 11:28-29

"For His anger is but for a moment, His favor is for a lifetime; weeping may last for the night, but a shout of joy comes in the morning."
Psalm 30:5

"To You, O LORD, I called, and to the Lord I made supplication: What profit is there in my blood, if I go down to the pit? Will the dust praise You? Will it declare Your faithfulness? Hear, O LORD, and be gracious to me; O LORD, be my helper.

"You have turned for me my mourning into dancing; You have loosed my sackcloth and girded me with gladness, that my soul may sing praise to You and not be silent. O LORD my God, I will give thanks to You forever."
Psalm 30:8-12

"Finally, brethren, whatever is true, whatever is honorable, whatever is right, whatever is pure, whatever is lovely, whatever is of good repute, if there is any excellence and if anything worthy of praise, dwell on these things."
Philippians 4:8

"For if you return to the LORD, your brothers and your sons will find compassion before those who led them captive and will return to this land. For the LORD your God is gracious and compassionate, and will not turn His face away from you if you return to Him."
2 Chronicles 30:9

"He has not dealt with us according to our sins, nor rewarded us according to our iniquities. For as high as the heavens are above the earth, so great is His loving kindness toward those who fear Him. As far as the east is from the west, so far has He removed our transgressions from us."
Psalm 103:10-12

"This hope we have as an anchor of the soul, a hope both sure and steadfast and one which enters within the veil."
Hebrews 6:19

"Let us not lose heart in doing good, for in due time we will reap if we do not grow weary."
Galatians 6:9

"The Spirit of the Lord GOD is upon me, because the LORD has anointed me to bring good news to the afflicted; He has sent me to bind up the brokenhearted, to proclaim liberty to captives and freedom to prisoners."
Isaiah 61:1

"He gives strength to the weary, and to him who lacks might He increases power. Though youths grow weary and tired, and vigorous young men stumble badly, yet those who wait for the LORD will gain new strength; they will mount up with wings like eagles, they will run and not get tired, they will walk and not become weary."
Isaiah 40:29-31

"He heals the brokenhearted and binds up their wounds."
Psalm 147:3

Doubt

Many Christians struggle with doubt. Doubts can be intellectual, where we doubt that the Bible is really inspired by God or that Jesus really resurrected from the dead. Doubts can also be emotional. When a person has experienced great sorrow or disappointment, such as the loss of a job, a divorce, or the death of a loved one, they might doubt the goodness, love, and care of their heavenly Father.

Whether intellectual or emotional, having doubts of any kind can be scary. It makes people wonder if their questions mean they are not a Christian. No one is immune to doubt. It can and does happen to us all. You've just got to know how to handle it when it comes. See Abraham in Genesis 17:17, Zechariah in Luke 1:20, and the Apostles in Luke 24:38, Luke 17:5.

There is a difference between unbelief and doubt. Unbelief is when people willfully set themselves against a biblical teaching. Doubt is when people have an intellectual or emotional barrier to a more solid faith in a biblical teaching or to God. Doubters want to believe, but they just need some help to believe. What is important is what you do with your doubt.

When we doubt God's goodness, it is not because God is not good, it is because we lack understanding. When we doubt that God is real, it is not because of a lack of evidence. It is because there is something blocking us from seeing all the evidence. At a fundamental level, I think many of us hide our doubts from God because we are worried that our doubt reveals some deficiency in God. Not so. It reveals a deficiency in us. That is why we need to admit it to God, like every other deficiency, so that he can help us with it. Pray and ask God for understanding.

Scripture references to help you deal with doubt:

"And Jesus answered saying to them, "Have faith in God. Truly I say to you, whoever says to this mountain, "Be taken up and cast into the sea," and does not doubt in his heart, but believe that what he says is going to happen, it will be granted him.

Therefore I say to you, all things for which you pray and ask, believe that you have received them, and they will be granted you."
Mark 11:22-24

"And do not seek what you will eat and what you will drink, and do not keep worrying. For all these things the nations of the world eagerly seek; but your Father knows that you need these things. But seek His kingdom, and these things will be added to you."

Spiritual Gifts

Unveiling Your Inner Light

Luke 12:29-31

"Yet, with respect to the promise of God, he did not waver in unbelief but grew strong in faith, giving glory to God, and being fully assured that what God had promised, He was able also to perform."
Romans 4:20-21

"Faithful is He who calls you, and He also will bring it to pass."
1 Thessalonians 5:24

"The Lord is not slow about His promise, as some count slowness, but is patient toward you, not wishing for any to perish but for all to come to repentance."
2 Peter 3:9

"As for God, His way is blameless; the word of the LORD is tried; He is a shield to all who take refuge in Him."
Psalm 18:30

"Behold, the LORD'S hand is not so short that it cannot save; nor is His ear so dull that it cannot hear."
Isaiah 59:1

"Beloved, do not be surprised at the fiery ordeal among you, which comes upon you for your testing, as though some strange thing were happening to you; but to the degree that you share the sufferings of Christ, keep on rejoicing, so that also at the revelation of His glory you may rejoice with exultation."
1 Peter 4:12-13

"So faith comes from hearing, and hearing by the word of Christ."
Romans 10:17

"For as the rain and the snow come down from heaven, and do not return there without watering the earth and making it bear and sprout, and furnishing seed to the sower and bread to the eater;

Spiritual Gifts _____

Unveiling Your Inner Light

So will My word be which goes forth from My mouth; it will not return to Me empty, without accomplishing what I desire, and without succeeding in the matter for which I sent it."
Isaiah 55:10-11

Fear

In the Bible, God says, "fear not" or is specifically addressed in the bible over 360 times, because He wants us to know that we can rely on Him. Imagine yourself having a fearless future; you can expect great things being part of your renewed life. We, as human beings are led to believe that fear is normal. In fact, we're told that fear is a natural survival mechanism, that it prevents us from doing dangerous, harm threatening things. However, I beg to differ. Most every day, I talk with someone who is afraid or anxious (which is generalized fear). Maybe you fear what people think of you, not having enough money, public speaking, flying, being far from home, Death…etc. In order to understand exactly what fear is, we should look at the definition of fear and then ask ourselves, what does the Bible say about fear? We must realize that fear is not only an emotion, it is also a spirit, which can become a stronghold in the mind or soul. Inordinate fear will not go away on its own, one must cast it out.

The Bible gives us resources to break free from fear in order to live an abundant life. No medication required! However, a dose of faith is required. Webster defines fear as, "An emotion or anxious feeling aroused by a real or imagined threat (usually accompanied by a desire to flee, comply or fight)".

Living in fear builds walls, which are designed to limit a person's capability. Also, you must realize fear is a foreign spirit that does not come from God. If you are ever afraid of something, you can have confidence that the fear is coming from Satan. A Christian's reborn spirit does not produce fear, so if fear comes, it is an attack of the enemy against your soul. Our enemy has an objective to introduce fear into your mind so it makes its way to your spirit. When this happens, he can bring his plans of ruin to manifest in your life.

There is a choice you must make as a believer as to how you will live. Will it be in faith or fear? Living in fear is all about self-preservation,

Spiritual Gifts _____

Unveiling Your Inner Light

while living fearless is about selflessness, putting your faith (trusting) God the Father.

Fear causes people to be afraid to take the next step for advancement, because they're afraid of more responsibility. Fear of failure often causes people to dismiss pursuing a wonderful idea. Others are paralyzed by fear when they get up in the morning, afraid to go about the routines of life. Fear is a magnet to demons who strike fear in the hearts of believers by sending intimidation to frighten them away from faithfulness in His Word. Accept the Lord's ability to preserve you. You don't have to know it all and you surely don't have the ability to fix it all.

The spirit of fear can affect every area of our life because it:

- Divides our minds.

- Slows down our productivity. Because we are distracted with worry, we can't give anything else our best efforts.

- Affects our personal relationships with others. It's hard to keep our anxieties to ourselves. When we're filled with fear, we burden those around us.

- Leads to unwise decisions. Those who are overly concerned about the future are prone to make hasty decisions to stop feeling uncertain.

- Steals our joy and peace. It's impossible for us to be worried and peaceful at the same time.

- Proves to be a terrible waste of time and energy. Uncertainty, frustration, and worry are exhausting and achieve nothing and can even have a devastating effect on our health.

- A tool used by an enemy to manipulate or intimidate others subjecting them to bondage.

You can ask Jesus to save you from all fear and be King of your life. Simply pray... "Jesus, I trust you with my life. I believe "You" laid down your life on the cross, were buried and resurrected so that I can be free to live life abundantly. Thank You for loving me and for the gift of everlasting life in peace. Below are scripture references to help you overcome your fears."

Overcoming your fears scriptures:

"Even though I walk through the valley of the shadow of death, I fear no evil, for You are with me; Your rod and Your staff, they comfort me."
Psalm 23:4

"For the wages of sin is death, but the free gift of God is eternal life in Christ Jesus our Lord."
Romans 6:23

"For God so loved the world, that He gave His only begotten Son, that whoever believes in Him shall not perish, but have eternal life. For God did not send the Son into the world to judge the world, but that the world might be saved through Him."
John 3:16-17

"For such is God, our God forever and ever; He will guide us until death."
Psalm 48:14

"For I am convinced that neither death, nor life, nor angels, nor principalities, nor things present, nor things to come, nor powers, nor height, nor depth, nor any other created thing, will be able to separate us from the love of God, which is in Christ Jesus our Lord."
Romans 8:38-39

"O Death, where is your victory? O Death, where is your sting? The sting of death is sin, and the power of sin is the law; but thanks be to God, who gives us the victory through our Lord Jesus Christ."
1 Corinthians 15:55-57

"He will swallow up death for all time, and the Lord God will wipe tears away from all faces..."

Spiritual Gifts

Unveiling Your Inner Light

Isaiah 25:8

"Since the children have flesh and blood, he too shared in their humanity so that by his death he might destroy him who holds the power of death -- that is, the devil -- and free those who all their lives were held in slavery by their fear of death."
Hebrews 2:14-15 (NIV)

"But God will redeem my soul from the grave; He will surely take me to himself."
Psalm 49:15

"My flesh and my heart may fail, but God is the strength of my heart and my portion forever."
Psalm 73:26

"The wicked is thrust down by his wrongdoing, but the righteous has a refuge when he dies."
Proverbs 14:32

"For the mind set on the flesh is death, but the mind set on the Spirit is life and peace."
Romans 8:6

Supply your needs

Whatever your needs are, God wants you to know that His supply will be there for you. You have His Word for it. He promises that He will supply all your needs, not just some. And He will supply all your needs according to and not out of His riches. This means that He lines up from A to Z all of His resources for your every need. Rejoice that you are rich "according to His riches in glory by Christ Jesus". This is far greater and more dependable than the temporal riches that you might have from any earthly source!

We must always remember that God is faithful. No matter if we feel discouraged or disheartened we must embrace the truth of God's faithfulness. If we focus on our problems and troubles instead of God's faithfulness, we are heading down the dangerous highway that leads to discouragement and unbelief. We must trust Him and know that he is faithful to us His children. He will Take care of us.

God does not promise here that He will supply all our desires or wishes, but He promises that He will supply, and fulfill all our needs. Some may read these words and think they need new pretty toys for their lives and pray for frivolous items while others seek God in earnest for guidance; for strength against temptation, for happiness in a marriage, or the need for employment. Sadly, many people still make this foolish exchange with desires for needs, surrendering spiritual wealth, while seeking financial fatness. If we seek God in earnest with our hearts and minds stayed on Him we can be encouraged, and comforted that our God will supply all our needs.

Scripture references for Supply:

"My God will supply all your needs according to His riches in glory in Christ Jesus."
Philippians 4:19

"I can do all things through Him who strengthens me."
Philippians 4:13

"In all these things we overwhelmingly conquer through Him who loved us."
Romans 8:37

"Let no one boast in men. For all things belong to you, whether Paul or Apollos or Cephas or the world or life or death or things present or things to come; all things belong to you, and you belong to Christ; and Christ belongs to God."
1 Corinthians 3:21-23

"If you abide in Me, and My words abide in you, ask whatever you wish, and it will be done for you."
John 15:7

Spiritual Gifts

Unveiling Your Inner Light

"In that day you will not question Me about anything. Truly, truly, I say to you, if you ask the Father for anything in My name, He will give it to you. Until now you have asked for nothing in My name; ask and you will receive, so that your joy may be made full."
John 16:23-24

"All things you ask in prayer, believing, you will receive."
Matthew 21:22

"Therefore I say to you, all things for which you pray and ask, believe that you have received them, and they will be granted you."
Mark 11:24

"Blessed be the God and Father of our Lord Jesus Christ, who has blessed us with every spiritual blessing in the heavenly places in Christ."
Ephesians 1:3

"Whatever we ask we receive from Him, because we keep His commandments and do the things that are pleasing in His sight."
1 John 3:22

"He made Him who knew no sin to be sin on our behalf, so that we might become the righteousness of God in Him."
2 Corinthians 5:21

"For to me, to live is Christ and to die is gain."
Philippians 1:21

"Therefore if anyone is in Christ, he is a new creature; the old things passed away; behold, new things have come."
2 Corinthians 5:17

"Now to Him who is able to do far more abundantly beyond all that we ask or think, according to the power that works within us, to Him be the glory in the church and in Christ Jesus to all generations forever and ever. Amen."
Ephesians 3:20-21

"God is able to make all grace abound to you, so that always having all sufficiency in everything, you may have an abundance for every good deed."
2 Corinthians 9:8

"Blessed be the Lord, who daily bears our burden, the God who is our salvation."
Psalm 68:19

Hope

Hope means "to desire something with confident expectation of its fulfillment." The state of Hopelessness has been aptly described as a type of "Hell on Earth" filled with endless despondency and despair. Today, more and more people are finding themselves alone and depressed, and few of us have not at one time or another felt the sting of despondency and despair. But Good news! Help is available. Not the kind the world has wherein it wishes for the best. It is one thing to wish, and quite another to have faith based on the promises of God.

Rest assured, God has plans for you. You can believe that. His plans are not intended to harm you, but to prosper you. Now, this does not mean that He plans to make you rich, but He does plan for you to have a secure future. God says that He has plans for you and He knows them, even if we do not. God knows your future and is planning it better than anyone else can, even ourselves.

In order to reap the benefits of the Christian life and to have protection, guidance, and comfort from the Holy Spirit, one must first be born again and become a child of God. The born again child of God has the unique privilege of talking to, and hearing from God, but this, the greatest resource available, is often neglected. We should always pray! Even in the darkest moments, when you don't feel His presence, or think you will never smile again, pray anyway, because He is there, He is listening, and is an "ever present help in time of trouble" (Psa 46:1)

What do you do when life is hard? Most people turn to the quickest

Spiritual Gifts

Unveiling Your Inner Light

way to end their pain, even if it isn't the wisest choice. But there is only one sure answer for your heartache and difficulty—almighty God. There are some circumstances that may leave you feeling as if you don't have a friend in the world. However isolated you may feel, understand that you're never alone. The Holy Spirit is with you. His primary reason for indwelling you is to live the life of Christ through you—helping you face every situation in a godly, victorious manner. He uses all of your heartaches and burdens to teach you about the love, wisdom, and power of God. He enables you to become the person God created you to be and to succeed in whatever God calls you to achieve.

Even if you reach what you consider to be your lowest point, God's word says He will never leave or forsake you (Matt 28:20). He will give you peace and comfort even in the worst of circumstances, then lead you through, over or around the muck and mire of your situation, and again set your feet on solid ground. Our God is the God of new beginnings, and with Him nothing is impossible. Whether you are very young, or considered to be very old, trust in Him because with Him it is always just the beginning.

You may even find yourself in such a situation like divorce, death of a spouse, loss of health, finances, or whatever, that may force you to begin all over again, but is that so bad? Trusting God in difficult times forces us to seek His guidance, and to trust in Him.

Hope in the Lord gives us strength. When we hope in Him, we find the confidence and strength to face any challenge that comes our way. Hope in the Lord teaches us patience. Society encourages us to solve our own problems. But when we face an impossible or hopeless situation,

we must learn to wait patiently on the Lord. We do not need to be anxious or worried. We can find peace in God's unfailing love for us. Hope in the Lord brings encouragement. You know that feeling you get at the end of a long week? The anticipation of the weekend lifts your spirits. Now think about stretching that weekend out for eternity. We can find encouragement and joy amid life's struggles because we know we will live forever with Jesus. That is why we are told to anticipate His glorious return (Titus 2:13).

Spiritual Gifts

Unveiling Your Inner Light

Scripture References about Hope:

"Why are you in despair, O my soul? And why have you become disturbed within me? Hope in God, for I shall yet praise Him, the help of my countenance and my God."
Psalm 42:11

"Who through Him are believers in God, who raised Him from the dead and gave Him glory, so that your faith and hope are in God."
1 Peter 1:21

"Therefore, prepare your minds for action, keep sober in spirit, fix your hope completely on the grace to be brought to you at the revelation of Jesus Christ."
1 Peter 1:13

"And everyone who has this hope fixed on Him purifies himself, just as He is pure."
1 John 3:3

"The wicked is thrust down by his wrongdoing, but the righteous has a refuge when he dies."
Proverbs 14:32

"Because of the hope laid up for you in heaven, of which you previously heard in the word of truth, the gospel."
Colossians 1:5

"To whom God willed to make known what is the riches of the glory of this mystery among the Gentiles, which is Christ in you, the hope of glory."
Colossians 1:27

"Be strong and let your heart take courage, all you who hope in the LORD."
Psalm 31:24

"For You are my hope; O Lord GOD, You are my confidence from my youth."
Psalm 71:5

"Blessed be the God and Father of our Lord Jesus Christ, who according to His great mercy has caused us to be born again to a living hope through the resurrection of Jesus Christ from the dead."
1 Peter 1:3

Power

The earliest manifestation of God's power is seen in the creation of the world in which we live. Throughout Scripture, the creation of the world is cited as a compelling testimony of the power of God. God is so powerful and great that our little minds at best cannot take it all in. God has revealed Himself in His word, the Bible, adequately enough to give us a vast unfolding idea of His power to do anything thought by man to be impossible. God's power has no boundary and is everlasting. He has a sovereign right arid authority over man. He can do with his creatures as he pleases.

God provides the power we need through Jesus' blood, the Scriptures, prayer, hope, love, and other Christians. No one needs to be lost. Anyone can overcome their past, achieve victory over sin, and become what God requires him/her to be. You can have God's power working in your life! The scriptures below will help you to understand the power of God.

Scriptures outlining God's Power:

"A wise man is strong, and a man of knowledge increases power."
Proverbs 24:5

"He gives strength to the weary, and to him who lacks might He increases power."
Isaiah 40:29

Spiritual Gifts

Unveiling Your Inner Light

"The angel answered and said to her, 'The Holy Spirit will come upon you, and the power of the Most High will overshadow you; and for that reason the holy Child shall be called the Son of God.'"
Luke 1:35

"Amazement came upon them all, and they began talking with one another saying, 'What is this message? For with authority and power He commands the unclean spirits and they come out.'"
Luke 4:36

"All the people were trying to touch Him, for power was coming from Him and healing them all."
Luke 6:19

"You will receive power when the Holy Spirit has come upon you; and you shall be My witnesses both in Jerusalem, and in all Judea and Samaria, and even to the remotest part of the earth."
Acts 1:8

"With great power the apostles were giving testimony to the resurrection of the Lord Jesus, and abundant grace was upon them all."
Acts 4:33

"For I am not ashamed of the gospel, for it is the power of God for salvation to everyone who believes, to the Jew first and also to the Greek."
Romans 1:16

"For the word of the cross is foolishness to those who are perishing, but to us who are being saved it is the power of God."
1 Corinthians 1:18

"For the kingdom of God does not consist in words but in power."
1 Corinthians 4:20

"We have this treasure in earthen vessels, so that the surpassing greatness of the power will be of God and not from ourselves."
2 Corinthians 4:7

"For the weapons of our warfare are not of the flesh, but divinely

powerful for the destruction of fortresses."
2 Corinthians 10:4

"He has said to me, 'My grace is sufficient for you, for power is perfected in weakness.' Most gladly, therefore, I will rather boast about my weaknesses, so that the power of Christ may dwell in me."
2 Corinthians 12:9

"That He would grant you, according to the riches of His glory, to be strengthened with power through His Spirit in the inner man."
Ephesians 3:16

"Finally, be strong in the Lord and in the strength of His might."
Ephesians 6:10

"For God has not given us a spirit of timidity, but of power and love and discipline. Therefore do not be ashamed of the testimony of our Lord or of me His prisoner, but join with me in suffering for the gospel according to the power of God."
2 Timothy 1:7-8

"Seeing that His divine power has granted to us everything pertaining to life and godliness, through the true knowledge of Him who called us by His own glory and excellence."
2 Peter 1:3

"Therefore behold, I am going to make them know—This time I will make them know My power and My might; and they shall know that My name is the LORD."
Jeremiah 16:21

"'Not by might nor by power, but by My Spirit,' says the LORD of hosts."
Zechariah 4:6

"For I am not ashamed of the gospel, for it is the power of God for salvation to everyone who believes, to the Jew first and also to the Greek."
Romans 1:16

Spiritual Gifts _____

Unveiling Your Inner Light

"For this very purpose I raised you up, to demonstrate My power in you, and that My name might be proclaimed throughout the whole earth."
Romans 9:17

"Now may the God of hope fill you with all joy and peace in believing, so that you will abound in hope by the power of the Holy Spirit."
Romans 15:13

"These are in accordance with the working of the strength of His might which He brought about in Christ, when he raised Him from the dead and seated Him at His right hand in the heavenly

places, far above all rule and authority and power and dominion, and every name that is named, not only in this age but also in the one to come."
Ephesians 1:20-21

"He is the radiance of His glory and the exact representation of His nature, and upholds all things by the word of His power. When He had made purification of sins, He sat down at the right hand of the Majesty on high."
Hebrews 1:3

"Who are protected by the power of God through faith for a salvation ready to be revealed in the last time."
1 Peter 1:5

Worry and Anxiety

Anxiety can be defined as an overwhelming sense of tension that fragments our thoughts and divides our minds. In our complex world, we will always have opportunities to fret or worry. But a few moments of stress—after hearing frightening news, for instance—are far different from a life controlled by anxiety. The Bible teaches us how to avoid letting worry take over our lives. While imprisoned in Rome, the apostle Paul wrote, "Be anxious for nothing, but in everything by prayer and supplication with thanksgiving let your requests be made known to God. And the peace of God, which surpasses all comprehension, will guard your hearts and your minds in Christ Jesus" (Phil. 4:6-7). He knew how to have peace and contentment, no matter his circumstances (Phil. 4:9).

Why is it so important that we learn to deal with anxiety? This emotion disrupts our thoughts,

preventing us from thinking clearly and making wise decisions. Our productivity decreases because worry wastes time and energy. Relationships with our spouses, families, coworkers, and friends suffer. Anxiety also affects us physically by contributing to a host of health problems. It can hinder marital intimacy and hamper our fellowship with God. Jesus told His disciples, "Do not worry then, saying, 'What will we eat?' or 'What will we drink?' or 'What will we wear for clothing?' . . . Do not worry about tomorrow; for tomorrow will care for itself. Each day has enough trouble of its own" (Matt. 6:31, 34).

When we as believers live with anxiety building up, you and I are essentially saying that we don't trust our heavenly Father to take care of us. How can believers overcome anxiety? By praying right (Phil. 4:6-7): Christians should pray in all circumstances and situations, not just about the "big things." If we neglect to talk to God about a particular area of our lives, it often leads to a larger problem. But instead of focusing exclusively on a list of requests, we should seek to adore and worship the Lord. God already knows our needs, and He has the power to supply them. More than anything else, the Father desires for us to build an intimate, trusting relationship with Him; a relationship free of worry and anxiety.

Believers should also pray specifically. "Lord, please bless them" is not sufficient. Instead of making a general request, we should ask God for a friend or family member's healing, protection, or spiritual growth. Make time to pray for others even when you are going through a difficult season of life. Focusing exclusively on your own problems—even in prayer—can cause you to dwell on them even more. Christians should cry out to the Lord in supplication. This word indicates a passionate outpouring of the heart in contrast to mere "lip service." David testified to the Lord's faithfulness to deliver the righteous when they called to Him (Ps. 34:17). And our Savior cried out in supplication to the Father just before the crucifixion (Heb. 5:7). As believers, we can trust that God will also answer our fervent prayers.

Lastly, we are also to pray "with thanksgiving." You and I are dependent on the Lord for our very lives. When God doesn't answer our prayer immediately—or He says no—we should continue to be grateful for all He has already given us. What believers dwell on has a direct effect on how anxious we feel. Instead of worrying about what the future will bring, try focusing on your relationship with the Lord. Seek His will regarding your goals and life's purpose—for today, tomorrow, and the distant future. Talk to Him about stressful situations, and ask Him to help you handle them in a godly manner. Remember that the Father loves you and wants to guide and direct your decisions.

God's people are to meditate on "whatever is true, whatever is honorable, whatever is right, whatever is pure, whatever is lovely, whatever is of good repute . . . [and] anything worthy of praise" (Phil. 4:8). The way we, as Christians, conduct ourselves in business, in recreation, and with our families should be consistent with this standard. If believers want to have victory over anxiety, we must not only pray correctly, but think rightly as well (Isa. 26:3).

In John 14:27, Jesus promised, "Peace I leave with you; My peace I give to you; not as the world

gives do I give to you. Do not let your heart be troubled, nor let it be fearful." As believers, we still face adversity, but God can give us supernatural peace in the midst of suffering. Children of God have the security of knowing that nothing happens unless He allows it. And the Lord promises to use difficult situations for our ultimate good (Rom. 8:28).

By living right (Phil. 4:9); Those who lead ungodly lives cannot experience lasting peace. And people who don't know the Lord have no hope of life after death (Matt. 7:23). They may mask their fears with drugs, alcohol, work, or some other distraction, but they are living with apprehension about their eternal future. In chapter four of Philippians, Paul wrote, "The things you have learned and received and heard and seen in me, practice these things, and the God of peace will be with you" (v. 9).

Only when our relationship with the Father is right can we truly be free from anxiety.

Scriptures to help deal with Worry or Anxiety:

"Peace I leave with you; My peace I give to you; not as the world gives do I give to you. Do not let your heart be troubled, nor let it be fearful."
John 14:27

"Casting all your anxiety on Him, because He cares for you."
1 Peter 5:7

"Do not let your heart be troubled; believe in God, believe also in Me."
John 14:1

"Be anxious for nothing, but in everything by prayer and supplication with thanksgiving let your requests be made known to God. And the peace of God, which surpasses all comprehension, will guard your hearts and your minds in Christ Jesus."
Philippians 4:6-7

"Let the peace of Christ rule in your hearts, to which indeed you were called in one body; and be thankful."
Colossians 3:15

"And my God will supply all your needs according to His riches in glory in Christ Jesus."
Philippians 4:19

"For this reason I say to you, do not be worried about your life, as to what you will eat or what you will drink; nor for your body, as to what you will put on. Is not life more than food, and the body more than clothing? "Look at the birds of the air, that they do not sow, nor reap nor gather into barns, and yet your heavenly Father feeds them. Are you not worth much more than they? "And who of you by being worried can add a single hour to his life?

Spiritual Gifts

Unveiling Your Inner Light

"And why are you worried about clothing? Observe how the lilies of the field grow; they do not toil nor do they spin, yet I say to you that not even Solomon in all his glory clothed himself like one of these.

"But if God so clothes the grass of the field, which is alive today and tomorrow is thrown into the furnace, will He not much more clothe you? You of little faith! "Do not worry then, saying, 'What will we eat?' or 'What will we drink?' or 'What will we wear for clothing?'"

"For the Gentiles eagerly seek all these things; for your heavenly Father knows that you need all these things."But seek first His kingdom and His righteousness, and all these things will be added to you.

"So do not worry about tomorrow; for tomorrow will care for itself. Each day has enough trouble of its own."
Matthew 6:25-34

"For the mind set on the flesh is death, but the mind set on the Spirit is life and peace"
Romans 8:6

"For we who have believed enter that rest, just as He has said, 'AS I SWORE IN MY WRATH, THEY SHALL NOT ENTER MY REST,' although His works were finished from the foundation of the world. . . . So there remains a Sabbath rest for the people of God."
Hebrews 4:3, 9

"Those who love Your law have great peace, and nothing causes them to stumble."
Psalm 119:165

"He who dwells in the shelter of the Most High will abide in the shadow of the Almighty. I will say to the LORD, 'My refuge and my fortress, My God, in whom I trust!'"
Psalm 91:1-2

"In peace I will both lie down and sleep, For You alone, O LORD, make me to dwell in safety."

Spiritual Gifts

Unveiling Your Inner Light

Psalm 4:8

"When you lie down, you will not be afraid; When you lie down, your sleep will be sweet."
Proverbs 3:24

"The steadfast of mind You will keep in perfect peace, Because he trusts in You."
Isaiah 26:3

Overcoming Difficulty

Everyone has troubles. We face problems, affliction, suffering, and hardship. We need strength, endurance, and patience. Troubles concern us, not just because hardship itself is a burden, but also because affliction can lead to spiritual temptations. We may become so discouraged that we blame God for our troubles, lose faith in Him, or begin to doubt His goodness and mercy. When facing hardship we may think, "I just can't hold out." We may convince ourselves that, to expect someone to continue under our circumstances without sinning, would be expecting the impossible. So we may justify ourselves for disobeying God. But consider the Bible teaching that we can endure. "God is our refuge and strength. A very present help in trouble" (Psalm 46:1). God has promised to help us endure, but we must make use of the help He provides. Below are scriptures which will help you overcome difficulties.

Scriptures for Overcoming Difficulties:

"And we know that God causes all things to work together for good to those who love God, to those who are called according to His purpose."
Romans 8:28

"For I am convinced that neither death, nor life, nor angels, nor principalities, nor things present, nor things to come, nor powers, nor height, nor depth, nor any other created thing, will be able to separate us from the love of God, which is in Christ Jesus our Lord."
Romans 8:38-39

"For this reason I also suffer these things, but I am not ashamed; for I know whom I have believed and I am convinced that He is able to guard what I have entrusted to Him until that day."
2 Timothy 1:12-13

"When you are cast down, you will speak with confidence, And the humble person He will save."
Job 22:29

"It is better to take refuge in the Lord than to trust in man."
Psalm 118:8

"So then, brethren, stand firm and hold to the traditions which you were taught, whether by word of mouth or by letter from us. Now may our Lord Jesus Christ Himself and God our Father, who has loved us and given us eternal comfort and good hope by grace, comfort and strengthen your hearts in every good work and word."
2 Thessalonians 2:15-17

"But the Lord is faithful, and He will strengthen and protect you from the evil one. We have confidence in the Lord concerning you, that you are doing and will continue to do what we command. May the Lord direct your hearts into the love of God and into the steadfastness of Christ."
2 Thessalonians 3:3-5

"Encourage the exhausted, and strengthen the feeble. Say to those with anxious heart, 'Take courage, fear not. Behold, your God will come with vengeance; The recompense of God will come, But He will save you.' Then the eyes of the blind will be opened And the ears of the deaf will be unstopped. Then the lame will leap like deer, and the tongue of the mute will shout for joy. For waters will break forth in the wilderness and streams in the Arabah."
Isaiah 35:3-6

"Do not fear, for I am with you; Do not anxiously look about you, for I am your God. I will strengthen you, surely I will help you, surely I will uphold you with My righteous right hand."
Isaiah 41:10

Spiritual Gifts

Unveiling Your Inner Light

"I cry aloud with my voice to the Lord; I make supplication with my voice to the Lord. I pour out my complaint before Him; I declare my trouble before Him. When my spirit was overwhelmed within me, You knew my path. In the way where I walk They have hidden a trap for me. Look to the right and see: For there is no one who regards me; There is no escape for me; no one cares for my soul. I cried out to You, O Lord; I said, "You are my refuge, My portion in the land of the living. Give heed to my cry, For I am brought very low; Deliver me from my persecutors, For they are too strong for me. Bring my soul out of prison, so that I may give thanks to Your name; The righteous will surround me, For You will deal bountifully with me."
Psalm 142:1-7

"Instruct those who are rich in this present world not to be conceited or to fix their hope on the uncertainty of riches, but on God, who richly supplies us with all things to enjoy. Instruct them to do good, to be rich in good works, to be generous and ready to share, storing up for themselves the treasure of a good foundation for the future, so that they may take hold of that which is life indeed."
1 Timothy 6:17-19

"This poor man cried, and the Lord heard him and saved him out of all his troubles. The angel of the Lord encamps around those who fear Him, and rescues them. O taste and see that the Lord is good; How blessed is the man who takes refuge in Him! O fear the Lord, you His saints; For to those who fear Him there is no want. The young lions do lack and suffer hunger; But they who seek the Lord shall not be in want of any good thing."
Psalm 34:6-10

"But if God so clothes the grass in the field, which is alive today and tomorrow is thrown into the furnace, how much more will He clothe you? You men of little faith! And do not seek what you will eat and what you will drink, and do not keep worrying. For all these things the nations of the world eagerly seek; but your Father knows that you need these things. But seek His kingdom, and these things will be added to you."
Luke 12:28-31

Spiritual Gifts

Unveiling Your Inner Light

"Be angry and yet do not sin; do not let the sun go down on your anger, and do not give the devil an opportunity."
Ephesians 4:26-27

"He who overcomes, I will grant to him to sit down with Me on My throne, as I also overcame and sat down with My Father on His throne."
Revelation 3:21

"Be of sober spirit, be on the alert. Your adversary, the devil, prowls around like a roaring lion, seeking someone to devour. But resist him, firm in your faith, knowing that the same experiences of suffering are being accomplished by your brethren who are in the world. After you have suffered for a little while, the God of all grace, who called you to His eternal glory in Christ, will Himself perfect, confirm, strengthen and establish you."
1 Peter 5:8-10

"If the foundations are destroyed, What can the righteous do? The Lord is in His holy temple; the Lord's throne is in heaven; His eyes behold, His eyelids test the sons of men. The Lord tests the righteous and the wicked, And the one who loves violence His soul hates. Upon the wicked He will rain snares; Fire and brimstone and burning wind will be the portion of their cup. For the Lord is righteous, He loves righteousness; The upright will behold His face."
Psalm 11:3-7

"But we have this treasure in earthen vessels, so that the surpassing greatness of the power will be of God and not from ourselves; we are afflicted in every way, but not crushed; perplexed, but not despairing; persecuted, but not forsaken; struck down, but not destroyed."
2 Corinthians 4:7-9

"Therefore we do not lose heart, but though our outer man is decaying, yet our inner man is being renewed day by day. For momentary, light affliction is producing for us an eternal weight of glory far beyond all comparison, while we look not at the things which are seen, but at the things which are not seen; for the things which are seen are temporal, but the things which are not seen are eternal."

Spiritual Gifts

Unveiling Your Inner Light

2 Corinthians 4:16-18

"So the ransomed of the Lord will return and come with joyful shouting to Zion, and everlasting joy will be on their heads. They will obtain gladness and joy, and sorrow and sighing will flee away."
Isaiah 51:11

"Be anxious for nothing, but in everything by prayer and supplication with thanksgiving let your requests be made known to God. And the peace of God, which surpasses all comprehension, will guard your hearts and your minds in Christ Jesus. Finally, brethren, whatever is true, whatever is honorable, whatever is right, whatever is pure, whatever is lovely, whatever is of good repute, if there is any excellence and if anything worthy of praise, dwell on these things."
Philippians 4:6-8

"Though I walk in the midst of trouble, You will revive me; You will stretch forth Your hand against the wrath of my enemies, And Your right hand will save me."
Psalm 138:7

"Do not let your heart be troubled; believe in God, believe also in Me."
John 14:1

"Peace I leave with you; My peace I give to you; not as the world gives do I give to you. Do not let your heart be troubled, nor let it be fearful."
John 14:27

"Therefore, do not throw away your confidence, which has a great reward. For you have need of endurance, so that when you have done the will of God, you may receive what was promised."
Hebrews 10:35-36

"For I am confident of this very thing, that He who began a good work in you will perfect it until the day of Christ Jesus."
Philippians 1:6

"Let us not lose heart in doing good, for in due time we will reap if we do not grow weary."
Galatians 6:9

"Be strong and let your heart take courage, All you who hope in the Lord."
Psalm 31:24

Healing

Of all the promises in the Bible, those concerning healing are the most difficult for us to understand. Our confusion is often caused by the sadness we feel if someone doesn't recover. However, our unbelief in God's ability, an ignorance of biblical teaching on the subject, and others' false claims of healing also add to our misunderstanding. Perhaps that's why many people immediately respond to sickness by seeking medical help instead of turning to God first. This doesn't mean going to the doctor isn't essential, but the Lord should never be our last resort when all else fails. Since He's the Great Physician, why don't we seek Him to begin with? God is still in the healing business, but He does it according to His will and timing. When the Lord delays, it's because He's focused on something more important than a healthy body. His goal is to help us learn to listen to Him, and sickness has a way of grabbing our attention. Through it, we learn what He wants to teach us.

The Lord never changes, and His purposes and ways remain consistent throughout the Bible. By examining Old Testament teachings, Jesus' ministry, and the apostles' role in healing, we can come to a greater understanding of God's willingness to intervene in our struggles. As I look at Healing in the Old Testament, the first mention of the Lord's healing power is found in Genesis 20:17-18 when He answered Abraham's prayer and healed Abimelech's household. Many years later when Abraham's descendants became a nation, God promised to remove sickness from their midst if they served Him (Ex. 23:25). From that point, their wellness as a people depended on their obedience to the Lord. When they rebelled, God disciplined them with illness (Ps. 106:13-15), but whenever they cried out to Him, He "sent His word and healed them" (Ps. 107:20). They were

Spiritual Gifts

Unveiling Your Inner Light

restored when they believed and heeded His Word.

In Isaiah 53:5, God told His people about the healing that would come through the Messiah's atonement for sin: "By His scourging we are healed." Even though this promise is ours as a result of Christ's sacrifice, it doesn't guarantee that the Lord will restore our health every time we ask. All the benefits of redemption don't come to us in this life—some are reserved for us in heaven. The biggest accomplishment of the cross was the healing of our separation from the Lord, which was caused by our sin.

Even though Jesus came to earth primarily to die for our sins, a major part of His ministry involved healing the sick. When teaching or traveling, He stopped to meet individual needs. Wherever He went, crowds of sick people formed around Him, and He took the time to heal many of them (Matt. 14:34-36). In order to understand this promise, we must recognize His purpose. Although Christ's love for mankind was a powerful motivation, the primary reason for His healing miracles was to demonstrate that He was the Son of God.

Jesus' main focus was always on the heart. When a paralytic was lowered through the roof, instead of immediately healing him, Christ said, "Your sins are forgiven" (Mark 2:5). The Lord dealt with his soul before restoring his body.

Although Christ has ascended to the Father, He's still healing people from heaven. Today, there are astonishing recoveries doctors can't explain. The Lord is still answering our prayers about health issues and has never stopped performing miracles. Despite His power, Jesus didn't heal every sick person in Israel. For example, when He visited His hometown, He couldn't perform many miracles because of the people's unbelief (Matt. 13:58). Like them, we also live in a society that doubts Jesus' ability to heal. Instead of following this line of negative thinking, Christians should expect God to do the unusual and wait for Him to act on our behalf.

After the ascension, the apostles carried on Christ's work, and curing people was part of their witness. For example, when Peter and John met a lame beggar at the temple, they both encouraged him to believe that

Christ could do the impossible, and He did (Acts 3:6-7). The apostle Paul's life also teaches us a great deal about how and why God restores us. Since Paul was such a prominent apostle, we'd expect him to play a major role in restoring the sick, but there is only one account of him doing so (Acts 28:8). Perhaps this is because Paul was called by God primarily to proclaim the gospel, not to heal people.

Because he was appointed to teach and explain divine truth, Paul's writings are our guide to understanding what God has to say about spiritual gifts and healing. The Lord has gifted some believers with faith to pray for the restoration of others (1 Cor. 12:9). The intercessors cannot heal anyone—only God can do that—but because of their great faith, the Lord answers their prayers and gives a gift of health to those who are sick.

Being an apostle didn't guarantee that Paul's prayers for wellness were always answered. At one point in his travels, he left a sick friend in another city (2 Tim. 4:20). He also struggled with his own health issues, so Luke, who was a physician, accompanied him. In 2 Corinthians 12:7-10, Paul described a trial that he called "a thorn in the flesh." Despite his entreaties and prayers, God didn't heal him, but He did explain the reason for his illness. Its purpose was to keep Paul from exalting himself. Also, God promised His grace was sufficient, and He gave the apostle both the strength to endure hardships and be content with his situation.

Whenever you experience sickness, your first thought should be to ask the Lord how He wants you to respond. He may tell you to trust Him for healing or lead you to get medical help. Paul did both. He sought healing from the Lord, trusted God's choice for his life, and relied on Luke's aid in times of suffering. The goal is to be God-conscious and realize that the One who saved you is walking with you through every illness. He will direct your steps if you set your mind on him.

Scriptures on Healing:

Then your light will break forth like the dawn, and your healing shall spring forth speedily: and your righteousness shall go before you;

Spiritual Gifts

Unveiling Your Inner Light

Isaiah 58:8

For I will restore you to health, and I will heal thee of thy wounds, declares the LORD;

Jeremiah 30:17

But unto you that fear my name shall the Sun of righteousness arise with healing in his wings; and ye shall go forth, and leap like calves released from the stall.

Malachi 4:2

When the evening came, they brought unto him many that were possessed with devils: and he cast out the spirits with his word, and healed all the sick: That it might be fulfilled which was spoken by Esaias the prophet, saying, He took up our infirmities, and carried our diseases.

Matthew 8:16-17

And Jesus went through all the cities and villages, teaching in their synagogues, and preaching the gospel, and healing every sickness and every disease among the people.

Matthew 9:35

Then he called his twelve disciples together, and gave them power and authority over all devils, and to cure diseases. And he sent them to preach the kingdom of God, and to heal the sick.

Luke 9:1-2

When you enter a town and are welcome, eat such things that are set before you: And heal the sick that are therein, and say unto them, The kingdom of God is near you.

Luke 10:8-9

I hope this book has been as blessing to you. If you don't get anything else out of this book, my hope is that you have a better understanding of whom Christ really is and that you recognize your spiritual gifts and operate from your gifts in order that you have a better quality of life in Christ.

Resources

Stanley, Charles F. The Glorious Journey. Nashville: Thomas Nelson Publishers, 1996.

Munroe, Myles In Pursuit of Purpose. Shippensburg: Destiny Image Publishers, 1992.

Meyers, Joyce Filled with the Spirit. New York: Warner Books, 2001.

Fortune, Don & Katie Discover Your God-Given Gifts. Grand Rapids: Chosen Books, 1987.

Brown, Patricia D. Spirit gifts Participant Workbook. Nashville: Abingdon Press, 1996.

Scripture references The Holy Bible. New International Version, NIV, Zondervan Publishing, 1973, 1978, 1984.

Scripture references The Holy Bible. New Revised Standard Version, NRSV, Nashville: Thomas Nelson Publishers, 1990.

Scripture references The Holy Bible. New American Standard, NAS, Nashville: Thomas Nelson Publishers, 1960, 1962, 1968, 1971, 1972, 1973, 1975, 1977.

Spiritual Gifts information from Various Internet Websites 2005, 2006, 2007, 2011, 2013, 2014.

Spiritual Gifts

Unveiling Your Inner Light

Notes:

Notes:

CPSIA information can be obtained
at www.ICGtesting.com
Printed in the USA
FFOW05n1422141114